FAMOUS SHERIFFS
=== and ===
WESTERN OUTLAWS

Skyhorse Publishing books may be purchased in bulk at special discounts for sales promotion, corporate gifts, fund-raising, or educational purposes. Special editions can also be created to specifications. For details, contact the Special Sales Department, Skyhorse Publishing, 307 West 36th Street, 11th Floor, New York, NY 10018 or info@skyhorsepublishing.com.

Skyhorse® and Skyhorse Publishing® are registered trademarks of Skyhorse Publishing, Inc.®, a Delaware corporation.

Visit our website at www.skyhorsepublishing.com

10

Library of Congress Cataloging-in-Publication Data is available on file.

ISBN 978-1-61608-542-1

Printed in the United States of America

FAMOUS SHERIFFS
and
WESTERN OUTLAWS

Incredible True Stories of Wild West Showdowns and Frontier Justice

William MacLeod Raine

Skyhorse Publishing

CONTENTS

	PAGE
DODGE	1
TEXAS AS WAS	24
THE ESTANCIA LAND GRANTS	45
A FORGOTTEN FILIBUSTER	59
TOM HORN	80
HELLDORADO	92
LAW WEST OF THE PECOS	116
THE "APACHE KID"	161
THE STORY OF BEECHER'S ISLAND	175
"BUCKY" O'NEILL	186
WHEN THE OUTLAW RODE IN OKLAHOMA	201
THE WAR FOR THE RANGE	217
CARRYING LAW INTO THE MESQUITE	236
THE HUNTING OF HARRY TRACY	253
"FOUR SIXES TO BEAT——"	273

FAMOUS SHERIFFS
and
WESTERN OUTLAWS

DODGE

A Story of the Old Hell-raising Trail's End Where the Colt Was King

IT WAS in the days when the new railroad was pushing through the country of the plains Indians that a drunken cowboy got on the train at a way station in Kansas. John Bender, the conductor, asked him for his ticket. He had none, but he pulled out a handful of gold pieces.

"I wantta—g-go to—h-hell," he hiccoughed.

Bender did not hesitate an instant. "Get off at Dodge. One dollar, please."

Dodge City did not get its name because so many of its citizens were or had been, in the Texas phrase, on the dodge. It came quite respectably by its cognomen. The town was laid out by A. A. Robinson, chief engineer of the Atchison, Topeka & Santa Fe, and it was called for Colonel Richard I. Dodge, commander of the post at Fort Dodge and one of the founders of the place. It is worth noting this, because it is one of the few respectable facts in the early history of the cowboy capital. Dodge was a wild and uncurried prairie wolf, and it howled every night and all night long. It was gay and young and lawless. Its sense of humour was exaggerated and worked overtime. The crack of the six-shooter punctuated its hilarity ominously. Those who dwelt there were the valiant vanguard of civilization. For good or bad they were strong and forceful, many of them generous and big-hearted in spite of their lurid lives. The town was a hive of energy. One might justly use many adjectives about it, but the word respectable is not among them.

There were three reasons why Dodge won the reputation of being the wildest town the country had ever seen. In 1872 it was the end of the track, the last jumping-off spot into the wilderness, and in the days when transcontinental railroads were building across the desert the temporary terminus was always a gathering place of roughs and scalawags. The payroll was large, and gamblers, gunmen, and thugs gathered for the pickings. This was true of Hays, Abilene, Ogalala, and Kit Carson. It was true of Las Vegas and Albuquerque.

A second reason was that Dodge was the end of the long trail drive from Texas. Every year hundreds of thousands of longhorns were driven up from Texas by cowboys scarcely less wild than the hill steers they herded. The great plains country was being opened, and cattle were needed to stock a thousand ranches as well as to supply the government at Indian reservations. Scores of these trail herds were brought to Dodge for shipment, and after the long, dangerous, drive the punchers were keen to spend their money on such diversions as the town could offer. Out of sheer high spirits they liked to shoot up the town, to buck the tiger, to swagger from saloon to gambling hall, their persons garnished with revolvers, the spurs on their high-heeled boots jingling. In no spirit of malice they wanted it distinctly understood that they owned the town. As one of them once put it, he was born high up on the Guadaloupe, raised on prickly pear, had palled with alligators and quarrelled with grizzlies.

Also, Dodge was the heart of the buffalo country. Here the hunters were outfitted for the chase. From here great quantities of hides were shipped back on the new railroad. R. M. Wright, one of the founders of the town and always one of its leading citizens, says that his firm alone shipped two hundred thousand hides in one season. He estimates the number of buffaloes in the country at more than twenty-five million, admitting that many as well informed as he put the figure at four times as many. Many times he and others travelled through the vast herds for days at a time without ever losing sight of them. The killing of buffaloes was easy, because the animals were so stupid. When one was shot they would mill round and round. Tom Nickson killed 120 in forty minutes; in a little more than a month he slaughtered 2,173 of them. With good luck a man could earn a hundred dollars a day. If he had bad luck he lost his scalp.

The buffalo was to the plains Indian food, fuel, and shelter. As long as there were plenty of buffaloes he was in Paradise. But he saw at once that this slaughter would soon exterminate the supply. He hated the hunter and battled against his encroachments. The buffalo hunter was an intrepid plainsman. He fought Kiowas, Comanches, and the Staked Plain Apaches, as well as the Sioux and the Arapahoe. Famous among these hunters were Kirk Jordan, Charles Rath, Emanuel Dubbs, Jack Bridges, and Curly Walker. Others even better known were the two Buffalo Bills (William Cody and William Mathewson) and Wild Bill.

These three factors then made Dodge: it was the end of the railroad, the terminus of the cattle trail from Texas, the centre of the buffalo trade. Together they made it "the beautiful bibulous Babylon of the frontier," in the words of the editor of the Kingsley *Graphic*. There was to come a time later when the bibulous Babylon fell on evil days and its main source of income was old bones. They were buffalo bones, gathered in wagons, and piled beside the track for shipment, hundreds and hundreds of carloads of them, to be used for fertilizer. (I have seen great quantities of such bones as far north as the Canadian Pacific line, corded for shipment to a factory.) It used to be said by way of derision that buffalo bones were legal tender in Dodge.

But that was in the far future. In its early years Dodge rode the wave of prosperity. Hays and Abilene and Ogalala had their day, but Dodge had its day and its night, too. For years it did a tremendous business. The streets were so blocked that one could hardly get through. Hundreds of wagons were parked in them, outfits belonging to freighters, hunters, cattlemen, and the government. Scores of camps surrounded the town in every direction. The yell of the cowboy and the weird oath of the bullwhacker and the mule skinner were heard in the land. And for a time there was no law nearer than Hays City, itself a burg not given to undue quiet and peace.

Dodge was no sleepy village that could drowse along without peace officers. Bob Wright has set it down that in the first year of its history twenty-five men were killed and twice as many wounded. The elements that made up the town were too diverse for perfect harmony. The freighters did not like the railroad graders. The soldiers at the fort fancied themselves as scrappers. The cowboys and the buffalo hunters did not fraternize a little bit. The result was that Boot Hill began to fill up. Its inhabitants were buried with their boots on and without coffins.

There was another cemetery, for those who died in their beds. The climate was so healthy that it would have been very sparsely occupied those first years if it had not been for the skunks. During the early months Dodge was a city of camps. Every night the fires flamed up from the vicinity of hundreds of wagons. Skunks were numerous. They crawled at night into the warm blankets of the sleepers and bit the rightful owners when they protested. A dozen men died from these bites. It was thought at first that the animals were a special variety, known as the hydrophobia skunk. In later years I have sat around Arizona camp fires and heard this subject discussed heatedly. The Smithsonian Institute, appealed to as referee, decided that there was no such species and that deaths from the bites of skunks were probably due to blood poisoning caused by the foul teeth of the animal.

In any case, the skunks were only one half as venomous as the gunmen, judging by comparative statistics. Dodge decided it had to have law in the community. Jack Bridges was appointed first marshal.

Jack was a noted scout and buffalo hunter, the sort of man who would have peace if he had to fight for it. He did his sleeping in the afternoon, since this was the quiet time of the day. Someone shook him out of slumber one day to tell him that cowboys were riding up and down Front Street shooting the windows out of buildings. Jack sallied out, old buffalo gun in hand. The cowboys went whooping down the street across the bridge toward their camp. The old hunter took a long shot at one of them and dropped him. The cowboys buried the young fellow next day.

There was a good deal of excitement in the cow camps. If the boys could not have a little fun without some old donker, an old vinegaroon who couldn't take a joke, filling them full of lead it was a pretty howdy-do. But Dodge stood pat. The coroner's jury voted it justifiable homicide. In future the young Texans were more discreet.

In the early days whatever law there was did not interfere with casualties due to personal differences of opinion provided the affair had no unusually sinister aspect.

The first wholesale killing was at Tom Sherman's dance hall. The affair was between soldiers and gamblers. It was started by a trooper named Hennessey, who had a reputation as a bad man and a bully. He was killed, as were several others. The officers at the fort glossed over the matter, perhaps because they felt the soldiers had been to blame.

One of the lawless characters who drifted into Dodge the first year was Billy Brooks. He quickly established a reputation as a killer. My old friend Emanuel Dubbs, a buffalo hunter who "took the hides off'n" many a bison, is authority for the statement that Brooks killed or wounded fifteen men in less than a month after his arrival. Now Emanuel is a preacher (if he is still in the land of the living; I saw him last at Clarendon, Texas, ten years or so ago), but I cannot quite swallow that "fifteen." Still, he had a man for breakfast now and then and on one occasion four.

Brooks, by the way, was assistant marshal. It was the policy of the officials of these wild frontier towns to elect as marshal some conspicuous killer, on the theory that desperadoes would respect his prowess or if they did not would get the worst of the encounter.

Abilene, for instance, chose "Wild Bill" Hickok. Austin had its Ben Thompson. According to Bat Masterson, Thompson was the most dangerous man with a gun among all the bad men he knew—and Bat knew them all. Ben was an Englishman who struck Texas while still young. He fought as a Confederate under Kirby Smith during the Civil War and under Shelby for Maximilian. Later he was city marshal at Austin. Thompson was a man of the most cool effrontery. On one occasion, during a cattlemen's convention, a banquet was held at the leading hotel. The local congressman, a friend of Thompson, was not invited. Ben took exception to this and attended in person. By way of pleasantry he shot the plates in front of the diners. Later one of those present made humorous comment. "I always thought Ben was a game man. But what did he do? Did he hold up the whole convention of a thousand cattlemen? No, sir. He waited till he got forty or fifty of us poor fellows alone before he turned loose his wolf."

Of all the bad men and desperadoes produced by Texas, not one of them, not even John Wesley Hardin himself, was more feared than Ben Thompson. Sheriffs avoided serving warrants of arrest on him. It is recorded that once, when the county court was in session with a charge against him on the docket, Thompson rode into the room on a mustang. He bowed pleasantly to the judge and court officials.

"Here I am, gents, and I'll lay all I'm worth that there's no charge against me. Am I right? Speak up, gents. I'm a little deaf."

There was a dead silence until at last the clerk of the court murmured, "No charge."

A story is told that on one occasion Ben Thompson met his match in the person of a young English remittance man playing cards with him. The remittance man thought he caught Thompson cheating and indiscreetly said so. Instantly Thompson's .44 covered him. For some unknown reason the gambler gave the lad a chance to retract.

"Take it back—and quick," he said grimly.

Every game in the house was suspended while all eyes turned on the dare-devil boy and the hard-faced desperado. The remittance man went white, half rose from his seat, and shoved his head across the table toward the revolver.

"Shoot and be damned. I say you cheat," he cried hoarsely.

Thompson hesitated, laughed, shoved the revolver back into its holster, and ordered the youngster out of the house.

Perhaps the most amazing escape on record is that when Thompson, fired at by Mark Wilson at a distance of ten feet from a double-barrelled shotgun loaded with buckshot, whirled instantly, killed him, and an instant later shot through the forehead Wilson's friend Mathews, though the latter had ducked behind the bar to get away. The second shot was guesswork plus quick thinking and accurate aim. Ben was killed a little later, in company with his friend King Fisher, another bad man, at the Palace Theatre. A score of shots were poured into them by a dozen men waiting in ambush. Both men had become so dangerous that their enemies could not afford to let them live.

King Fisher was the humorous gentleman who put up a signboard at the fork of a public road bearing the legend:

THIS IS KING FISHER'S ROAD. TAKE THE OTHER

It is said that those travelling that way followed his advice. The other road might be a mile or two farther, but they were in no hurry. Another amusing little episode in King Fisher's career is told. He had had some slight difficulty with a certain bald-headed man. Fisher shot him and carelessly gave the reason that he wanted to see whether a bullet would glance from a shiny pate.

El Paso in its wild days chose Dallas Stoudenmire for marshal, and after he had been killed, John Selman. Both of them were noted killers. During Selman's régime John Wesley Hardin came to town. Hardin had twenty-seven notches on his gun and was the worst man killer Texas had ever produced. He was at the bar of a saloon shaking dice when Selman shot him from behind. One year later Deputy United States Marshal George Scarborough killed Selman in a duel. Shortly after this Scarborough was slain in a gun fight by "Kid" Curry, an Arizona bandit.

What was true of these towns was true, too, of Albuquerque and Las Vegas and Tombstone. Each of them chose for peace officers men who were "sudden death" with a gun. Dodge did exactly the same thing. Even a partial list of its successive marshals reads like a fighting roster. In addition to Bridges and Brooks may be named Ed and Bat Masterson, Wyatt Earp, Billy Tilghman, Ben Daniels, Mysterious Dave Mathers, T. C. Nixon, Luke Short, Charley Bassett, W. H. Harris, and the Sughrue brothers, all of them famous as fighters in a day when courage and proficiency with weapons were a matter of course. On one occasion the superintendent of the Santa Fe suggested to the city dads of Dodge that it might be a good thing to employ marshals less notorious. Dodge begged leave to differ. It felt that the best way to "settle the hash" of desperadoes was to pit against them fighting machines more efficient, bad men more deadly than themselves.

The word "bad" does not necessarily imply evil. One who held the epithet was known as one dangerous to oppose. He was unafraid, deadly with a gun, and hard as nails. He might be evil, callous, treacherous, revengeful as an Apache. Dave Mathers fitted this description. He might be a good man, kindly, gentle, never taking more than his fighting chance. This was Billy Tilghman to a T.

We are keeping Billy Brooks waiting. But let that go. Let us look first at "Mysterious Dave." Bob Wright has set it down that Mathers had more dead men to his credit than any other man in the West. He slew seven by actual count in one night, in one house, according to Wright. Mather had a very bad reputation. But his courage could blaze up magnificently. While he was deputy marshal word came that the Henry gang of desperadoes were terrorizing a dance hall. Into that hall walked Dave, beside his chief Tom Carson. Five minutes later out reeled Carson, both arms broken, his body shot through and through, a man with only minutes to live. When the smoke in the hall cleared away Mathers might have been seen beside two handcuffed prisoners, one of them wounded. In a circle round him were four dead cowpunchers of the Henry outfit.

"Uncle" Billy Tilghman died the other day at Cromwell, Oklahoma, a victim of his own fearlessness. He was shot to death while taking a revolver from a drunken prohibition agent. If he had been like many other bad men he would have shot the fellow down at the first sign of danger. But that was never Tilghman's way. It was his habit to make arrests without drawing a gun. He cleaned up Dodge during the three years while he was marshal. He broke up the Doolin gang, killing Bill Raidler and "Little" Dick in personal duels and capturing Bill Doolin the leader. Bat Masterson said that during Tilghman's terms as sheriff of Lincoln County, Oklahoma, he killed, captured, or drove from the country more criminals than any other official that section ever had. Yet "Uncle" Billy never used a gun except reluctantly. Time and again he gave the criminal first shot, hoping the man would surrender rather than fight. Of all the old frontier sheriffs none holds a higher place than Billy Tilghman.

After which diversion we return to Billy Brooks, a "gent" of an impatient temperament, not used to waiting, and notably quick on the trigger. Mr. Dubbs records that late one evening in the winter of '72–'73 he returned to Dodge with two loads of buffalo meat. He finished his business, ate supper, and started to smoke a postprandial pipe. The sound of a fusillade in an adjoining dance hall interested him since he had been deprived of the pleasures of metropolitan life for some time and had had to depend upon Indians for excitement. (Incidentally, it may be mentioned that they furnished him a reasonable amount. Not long after this three of his men were caught, spread-eagled, and tortured by Indians. Dubbs escaped after a hair-raising ride and arrived at Adobe Walls in time to take part in the historic defence of that post by a handful of buffalo hunters against many hundred tribesmen.) From the building burst four men. They started across the railroad track to another dance hall, one frequented by Brooks. Dubbs heard the men mention the name of Brooks, coupling it with an oath. Another buffalo hunter named Fred Singer joined Dubbs. They followed the strangers, and just before the four reached the dance hall Singer shouted a warning to the marshal. This annoyed the unknown four, and they promptly exchanged shots with the buffalo hunters. What then took place was startling in the sudden drama of it.

Billy Brooks stood in bold relief in the doorway, a revolver in each hand. He fired so fast that Dubbs says the sound was like a company discharging weapons. When the smoke cleared Brooks still stood in the same place. Two of the strangers were dead and two mortally wounded. They were brothers. They had come from Hays City to avenge the death of a fifth brother shot down by Brooks some time before.

Mr. Brooks had a fondness for the fair sex. He and Browney, the yard master, took a fancy to the same girl. Captain Drew, she was called, and she preferred Browney. Whereupon Brooks naturally shot him in the head. Perversely, to the surprise of everybody, Browney recovered and was soon back at his old job.

Brooks seems to have held no grudge at him for making light of his marksmanship in this manner. At any rate, his next affair was with Kirk Jordan, the buffalo hunter.

This was a very different business. Jordan had been in a hundred tight holes. He had fought Indians time and again. Professional killers had no terror for him. He threw down his big buffalo gun on Brooks, and the latter took cover. Barrels of water had been placed along the principal streets for fire protection. These had saved several lives during shooting scrapes. Brooks ducked behind one, and the ball from Jordan's gun plunged into it. The marshal dodged into a store, out of the rear door, and into a livery stable. He was hidden under a bed. Alas! for a large reputation gone glimmering. Mr. Brooks fled to the fort, took the train from the siding, and shook forever the dust of Dodge from his feet. Whither he departed deponent sayeth not.

How do I explain this? I don't. I record a fact. Many gunmen were at one time or another subject to these panics during which the yellow streak showed. Not all of them by any means, but a very considerable percentage. They swaggered boldly, killed recklessly. Then one day some quiet little man with a cold gray eye called the turn on them, after which they oozed out of the surrounding scenery.

Owen P. White gives it on the authority of Charlie Siringo that Bat Masterson sang small when Clay

Allison of the Panhandle, he of the well-notched gun, drifted into Dodge and inquired for the city marshal. But the old-timers at Dodge do not bear this out. Bat was at the Adobe Walls fight, one of fourteen men who stood off five hundred bucks of the Cheyenne, Comanche, and Kiowa tribes. He scouted for Miles. He was elected sheriff of Ford County, with headquarters at Dodge, when only twenty-two years of age. It was a tough assignment, and Bat executed it to the satisfaction of all concerned except the element he cowed.

Personally, I never met Bat until his killing days were past. He was dealing faro at a gambling house in Denver when I, a young reporter, first had the pleasure of looking into his cold blue eyes. It was a notable fact that all the frontier bad men had eyes either gray or blue, often a faded blue, expressionless, hard as jade.

It is only fair to Bat to say that the old-timers of Dodge do not accept the Siringo point of view about him. Wright said of him that he was absolutely fearless and no trouble hunter. "Bat is a gentleman by instinct, of pleasant manners, good address, and mild until aroused, and then, for God's sake, look out. He is a leader of men, has much natural ability, and good hard common sense. There is nothing low about him. He is high-toned and broad-minded, cool and brave." I give this opinion for what it is worth.

In any case, he was a most efficient sheriff. Dave Rudabaugh, later associated with Billy the Kid in New Mexico, staged a train robbery at Kinsley,

Kansas, a territory not in Bat's jurisdiction. However, Bat set out in pursuit with a posse. A near-blizzard was sweeping the country. Bat made for Lovell's cattle camp, on the chance that the bandits would be forced to take shelter there. It was a good guess. Rudabaugh's outfit rode in, stiff and half frozen, and Bat captured the robbers without firing a shot. This was one of many captures Bat made.

He had a deep sense of loyalty to his friends. On two separate occasions he returned to Dodge, after having left the town, to straighten out difficulties for his friends or to avenge them. The first time was when Luke Short, who ran a gambling house in Dodge, had a difficulty with Mayor Webster and his official family. Luke appears to have held the opinion that the cards were stacked against him and that this was a trouble out of which he could not shoot himself. He wired Bat Masterson and Wyatt Earp to come to Dodge. They did, accompanied by another friend or two. The mayor made peace on terms dictated by Short.

Bat's second return to Dodge was caused by a wire from his brother James, who ran a dance hall in partnership with a man named Peacock. Masterson wanted to discharge the bartender, Al Updegraph, a brother-in-law of the other partner. A serious difficulty loomed in the offing. Wherefore James called for help. Bat arrived at eleven one sunny morning, another gunman at heel. At three o'clock he entrained for Tombstone, Arizona, James beside him. The interval had been a busy one. On the way up from the station (always known then as the depot), the two men met Peacock and Updegraph. No amenities were exchanged. It was strictly business. Bullets began to sing at once. The men stood across the street from each other and emptied their weapons. Oddly enough, Updegraph was the only one wounded. This little matter attended to, Bat surrendered himself, was fined three dollars for carrying concealed weapons, and released. He ate dinner, disposed of his brother's interest in the saloon, and returned to the station.

Bat Masterson was a friend of Theodore Roosevelt, who was given to admiring men with "guts," such men as Pat Garrett, Ben Daniels, and Billy Tilghman. Mr. Roosevelt offered Masterson a place as United States Marshal of Arizona. The ex-sheriff declined it. "If I took it," he explained, "inside of a year I'd have to kill some fool boy who wanted to get a reputation by killing me." The President then offered Bat a place as Deputy United States Marshal of New York, and this was accepted. From that time Masterson became a citizen of the Empire State. For seventeen years he worked on a newspaper there and died a few years since with a pen in his hand. He was respected by the entire newspaper fraternity.

Owing to the pleasant habit of the cowboys of shooting up the town they were required, when entering the city limits, to hand over their weapons to the marshal. The guns were deposited at Wright & Beverly's store, in a rack built for the purpose, and receipts given for them. Sometimes a hundred six-shooters would be there at once. These were never returned to their owners unless the cowboys were sober.

To be a marshal of one of these fighting frontier towns was no post to be sought for by a supple politician. The place called for a chilled iron nerve and an uncanny skill with the Colt. Tom Smith, one of the gamest men and best officers who ever wore a star on the frontier, was killed in the performance of his duty. Colonel Breakenridge says that Smith, marshal at Abilene before "Wild Bill," was the gamest man he ever knew. He was a powerful, athletic man who would arrest, himself unarmed, the most desperate characters. He once told Breakenridge that anyone could bring in a dead man but it took a good officer to take lawbreakers while they were alive. In this he differed from Hickok who did not take chances. He brought his men in dead. Nixon, assistant marshal at Dodge, was murdered by "Mysterious Dave" Mather, who himself once held the same post. Ed Masterson, after displaying conspicuous courage many times, was mortally wounded April 9, 1878, by two desperate men, Jack Wagner and Alf Walker, who were terrorizing Front Street. Bat reached the scene a few minutes later and heard the story. As soon as his brother had died Bat went after the desperadoes, met them, and killed them both. The death of Ed Masterson shocked the town. Civic organizations passed resolutions of respect. During the funeral, which was the largest ever held in Dodge, all business houses were closed. It is not on record that anybody regretted the demise of the marshal's assassins.

Among those who came to Dodge each season to meet the Texas cattle drive were Ben and Bill Thompson, gamblers who ran a faro bank. Previously they had been accustomed to go to Ellsworth, while that point was the terminus of the drive. Here they had ruled with a high hand, killed the sheriff, and made their getaway safely. Bill got into a shooting affray at Ogalala. He was badly wounded and was carried to the hotel. It was announced openly that he would never leave town alive. Ben did not dare to go to Ogalala, for his record there had outlawed him. He came to Bat Masterson.

Bat knew Bill's nurse and arranged a plan of campaign. A sham battle was staged at the big dance hall, during the excitement of which Bat and the nurse carried the wounded man to the train, got him to a sleeper, and into a bed. Buffalo Bill met them next day at North Platte. He had relays of teams stationed on the road, and he and Bat guarded the sick man during the long ride, bringing him safely to Dodge.

Emanuel Dubbs ran a roadhouse not far from Dodge about this time. He was practising with his six-shooter one day when a splendidly built young six-footer rode up to his place. The stranger watched him as he fired at the tin cans he had put on fence posts. Presently the young fellow suggested he throw a couple of the cans up in the air. Dubbs did so.

Out flashed the stranger's revolvers. There was a roar of exploding shots. Dubbs picked up the cans. Four shots had been fired. Two bullets had drilled through each can.

"Better not carry a six-shooter till you learn to shoot," Bill Cody suggested, as he put his guns back into their holsters. "You'll be a living temptation to some bad man."

Buffalo Bill was on his way back to North Platte.

Life at Dodge was not all tragic. The six-shooter roared in the land a good deal, but there were very many citizens who went quietly about their business and took no part in the night life of the town. It was entirely optional with the individual. The little city had its legitimate theatres as well as its hurdy-gurdy houses and gambling dens. There was the Lady Gay, for instance, a popular vaudeville resort. There were well-attended churches. But Dodge boiled so with exuberant young life, often inflamed by bad liquor, that both theatre and church were likely to be the scenes of unexpected explosions.

A drunken cowboy became annoyed at Eddie Foy. While the comedian was reciting "Kalamazoo in Michigan" the puncher began bombarding the frail walls from outside with a .45 Colt's revolver. Eddie made a swift strategic retreat. A deputy marshal was standing near the cowpuncher, who was astride a plunging horse. The deputy fired twice. The first shot missed. The second brought the rider down. He was dead before he hit the ground. The deputy apologized later for his marksmanship, but he added by way of explanation, "The bronc sure was sun-fishin' plenty."

The killing of Miss Dora Hand, a young actress of much promise, was regretted by everybody in Dodge. A young fellow named Kennedy, the son of a rich cattleman, shot her unintentionally while he was trying to murder James Kelly. He fled. A posse composed of Sheriff Masterson, William Tilghman, Wyatt Earp, and Charles Bassett took the trail. They captured the man after wounding him desperately. He was brought back to Dodge, recovered, and escaped. His pistol arm was useless, but he used the other well enough to slay several other victims before someone made an end of him.

The gay good spirits of Dodge found continual expression in practical jokes. The wilder these were the better pleased was the town. "Mysterious Dave" was the central figure in one. An evangelist was conducting a series of meetings. He made a powerful magnetic appeal, and many were the hard characters who walked the sawdust trail. The preacher set his heart on converting Dave Mathers, the worst of bad men and a notorious scoffer. The meetings prospered. The church grew too small for the crowds and adjourned to a dance hall. Dave became interested. He went to hear Brother Johnson preach. He went a second time and a third. "He certainly preaches like the Watsons an' goes for sin all spraddled out," Dave conceded. Brother Johnson grew hopeful. It seemed possible that this brand could be snatched from the burning. He preached directly at Dave, and Dave buried his head in his hands and sobbed. The preacher said he was willing to die if he could convert this one vile sinner. Others of the deacons agreed that they, too, would not object to going straight to heaven with the knowledge that Dave had been saved.

"They were right excited an' didn't know straight up," an old-timer explained. "Dave, he looked so whipped his ears flopped. Finally he rose, an' said, 'I've got yore company, friends. Now, while we're all saved I reckon we better start straight for heaven. First off, the preacher; then the deacons; me last.' Then Dave whips out a whoppin' big gun an' starts shootin'. The preacher went right through a window an' took it with him. He was sure in some hurry. The deacons hunted cover. Seemed like they was willin' to postpone taking that through ticket to heaven. After that they never did worry any more about Dave's soul."

Many rustlers gathered around Dodge in those days. The most notorious of these was a gang of more than thirty under the leadership of Dutch Henry and Tom Owens, two of the most desperate outlaws ever known in Kansas. A posse was organized to run down this gang under the leadership of Dubbs, who had lost some of his stock. Before starting, the posse telephoned Hays City to organize a company to head off the rustlers. Twenty miles west of Hays the posse overtook the rustlers. A bloody battle ensued, during which Owens and several other outlaws were killed and Dutch Henry wounded six times. Several of the posse were also shot. The story has a curious sequel. Many years later, when Emanuel Dubbs was county judge of Wheeler County, Texas, Dutch Henry came to his house and stayed there several days. He was a thoroughly reformed man. Not many years ago Dutch Henry died in Colorado. He was a man with many good qualities. Even in his outlaw days he had many friends among the law-abiding citizens.

After the battle with the Henry-Owens gang rustlers operated much more quietly, but they did not cease stealing. One night three men were hanged to a cottonwood on Saw Log Creek, ten or twelve miles from Dodge. One of these was a young man of a good family who had drifted into rustling and had been carried away by the excitement of it. Another of the three was the son of Tom Owens. To this day the place is known as Horse Thief Cañon.

During its years of prosperity many eminent men visited Dodge, including Generals Sherman and Sheridan, President Hayes, and General Miles. Its reputation had extended far and wide. It was the wild and woolly cowboy capital of the Southwest, a place to quicken the blood of any man. Nearly all that gay, hard-riding company of cowpunchers, buffalo hunters, bad men, and pioneers have vanished into yesterday's seven thousand years. But certainly Dodge once had its day and its night of glory. No more rip-roaring town ever bucked the tiger.

TEXAS AS WAS

*A True Story of a Cattle Feud in the Days
When Desperate Men Rode No Man's Land
and Law Was in the Holster*

THE stage driver was a tanned, weather-beaten little
Westerner with faded blue eyes and long drooping
moustache. The most unassuming of men, the least
conspicuous, he looked at first sight the last person I
should have picked as the survivor of an adventure
so grim and desperate that it stands in a class by
itself even on the frontier where life or death used so
often to hang balanced by a hair. Yet the claim to
this unique distinction might fairly have been made
by George Marlow and by his brother Charles. Twice,
entirely unarmed, once in a prison cell and again in
the open shackled two by two, the Marlows were attacked by mobs fully equipped with Winchesters
and Colts. Each time they drove back the would-be
lynchers, leaving in all half a dozen dead and as
many wounded on the fields of battle. It is an incredible tale—but it happens to be true.

Certainly this gentle, apologetic little fellow in
dusty gray jeans and pinched-in Stetson did not look
the part of hero (or villain if you take that point of

view) of a drama so stark and bloody. But I remembered that the fighting men of the old West rarely filled the eye satisfactorily. The fierce, long-haired bullies were usually false alarms.

"Box seat taken?" I inquired.

"No, seh."

"Then it's mine."

"Just as you say, stranger."

His whip snaked out, and the small horses jumped to a trot. I found the old-timer companionable in the silent, friendly way of the plainsman, but when I ventured an allusion to the story of the Dry Creek battle he entered a demurrer.

"Ain't it time we buried that ancient history, friend?" he asked in his slow drawl.

It was not such ancient history then as it is now, for that was twenty years ago. In Colorado, in Oklahoma, in Texas were scores of scattered cattlemen who recalled the story vividly. Some of them carried scars as mementoes of it. To-day not so many will remember it. For time has taken its toll of the pioneers.

The stage set for the drama was on the Brazos River, at Graham, Young County, Texas, the scene of more than one bloody feud. Here within a decade or two hardy settlers had fought it out with Kiowas and Comanches to hold the land they had squatted upon. The buffalo had been swept away, and the longhorn had drifted westward. Most of the early feuds had their genesis in disputes over cattle. According to the Marlows, the trouble here was between the large and the small cattle owners. Those on the other side tell another story. The five Marlow brothers, according to them, were rustlers and bad men. They had operated for years, not only in Texas, but in Colorado and the Indian Territory.

During the latter 'eighties the Marlows shifted frequently the locale of their operations. They were cowpunchers, cattlemen in a small way. Charges were made that they had stolen horses both in Colorado and in the Indian Territory, which was then a resort for the wildest and most lawless characters. It is sure that the Marlows spent a good deal of time in the Territory. There is a station on the Rock Island railroad to-day named Marlow. The little town lies on the border between the old Chickasaw Nation and the territory occupied by the Kiowas, Comanches, and Apaches. It was a convenient location for men on the dodge, for men who rode by night, flitting inconspicuously back and forth as their dubious business called them. The Dan Wagner cow outfit was a large one, covering a wide sweep of territory leased from the Indian Department. Many a nester fattened his small herd at the expense of the big brand.

Most of the Marlow brothers married, but the family tie was strong, or else there was safety in numbers. They kept in close touch with each other until an unfortunate incident temporarily divided them. One of the brothers, Boone by name, had a difference with James Holdson, as a result of which the latter was buried and the former slapped a saddle on his bronco and vanished. This took place in Wilbarger County, Texas. The neighbours resented it so much that the Marlows pulled up stakes again and drifted to Las Animas County, Colorado.

If they were honest men they were very unlucky. They left Trinidad under a cloud. From the sheriff of Las Animas County, known as "Doc" Burns, a telegram went to Deputy United States Marshal Ed. W. Johnson. It said:

Look out for five Marlow brothers trying to get away with forty head of horses stolen near here.

Johnson was a typical Westerner, large, rawboned, with keen eyes and square jaw. A year prior to this time he had lost one of his hands in a shooting affray. There was a rumour, possibly propagated by his enemies, that he had been appointed to represent the big cattle interests, which recently had formed an association to prevent cattle rustling as well as to check the bands of thieves and murderers that drifted down occasionally from the Territory. The Marlows claimed later that he pigeonholed a second telegram from Sheriff Burns mentioning that the horses had been found. To support this charge I have seen no evidence.

In any case, Johnson acted with energy. It looked reasonable to him that the Marlows would head for the Nation. There the horses could be traded to the Indians with no questions asked. Possession would be considered title of ownership. He wrote letters, received answers, and presently left for the North. Apparently the Marlows had no suspicion that the law was close on their heels. They were taking it easy among their friends in the Indian country when Johnson's posse unexpectedly arrived. Boone and Lewellyn (generally called Epp) were husking corn when they heard the crisp summons, "Hands up!" Resistance was out of the question. They surrendered. Alfred and Charley were surprised at the place of Old Sunday Boy, an Indian chief with whom they did business. The four brothers were taken by Johnson to Fort Sill. This was on August 29, 1888.

A clipping from the Graham *Leader*, issue of September 6, 1888, may serve to show the reputation of the arrested men.

Deputy Marshal E. W. Johnson and posse returned from the Indian Territory Tuesday evening, having in custody Alf, Charles, Epp, and Boone Marlow, who are charged with horse stealing in the Territory and Trinidad, Colorado. Boone Marlow is also wanted in Wilbarger County for the murder of Holdson in 1886. . . . The Marlow brothers are desperate characters and have been in the horse business in the Territory for six years. They had in possession a goodly number of the best Sharp's rifles, and if Mr. Johnson had failed to get the drop on them they would no doubt have made it lively for the posse.

The *Leader* of October 11th mentions that Marshal Johnson had returned again with more prisoners. Some of these were cow thieves. George Marlow and his nephew Bill Murphy, among the catch, were wanted for horse stealing. George had been arrested at Anadorka, thirty-six miles from Fort Sill.

By giving stock as security Mrs. Marlow, the mother of the five men, succeeded in getting them freed pending a trial.

Rustlers had been growing very bold in their operations. It was claimed by the Marlows that the big cattlemen determined to make an example of them to intimidate other offenders. An indictment was drawn up accusing the Marlows of stealing one hundred and thirty head of horses from the Indians, but the evidence supporting this was not sufficient to convict, and it was abandoned.

By way of parenthesis it may be said that though the Marlows were many times accused of rustling, though they were frequently arrested, indicted, and several times tried, there does not appear to be any conviction on record against them. This does not necessarily imply innocence. Even to-day it is very hard to get convincing evidence against rustlers, though cattle detectives make life difficult for the thieves. It is only fair to add that in those days of rather free and easy ownership the branding of another man's calf was rather a casual offence. Many of the big cattlemen had used a running iron freely themselves in the days before they achieved respectability and a large herd.

The movement of the drama quickened now. On Saturday, December 15th, Boone Marlow was released. Sunday there reached Sheriff Marion D. Wallace of Young County a capias for the arrest of Boone from the district court of Wilbarger County on the charge of murdering Holdson. Next day Wallace, with his deputy Tom Collier, rode out to the Marlow place to make the arrest.

Boone, Charley, and Epp were at dinner with their wives and their mother. Wallace swung from the saddle at the chimney end of the cabin, where there was neither door nor window, and stopped to tie his horse. Without dismounting, Collier rode forward, stooped down, and looked through the window.

Instantly Boone was on the alert, but he masked his wariness with a friendly hospitality. " 'Lo, Tom. Light an' rest yore saddle. Come in an' have some dinner."

"Reckon I won't eat," Collier answered as he left the saddle and dropped the reins.

The two officers entered the cabin.

"We want you, Boone," the sheriff said.

Boone had backed to the corner of the cabin where his rifle was. He seized it and fired. The ball passed through Collier's hat, just grazing his temple. A second shot struck the sheriff just above the hip, passing through his body. Collier fired his pistol and missed.

Wallace staggered back and dropped down on the porch. The deputy retreated to the end of the house. The brothers of Boone claimed that he wanted to kill the deputy but that they restrained him almost by force. The homicidal moment passed. The Marlows called to Collier to drop his weapon, return, and wait upon his wounded friend.

The sheriff was carried into the house. His wounds were dressed by the women. One of the boys rode to Graham for a doctor and was at once arrested. Meanwhile, Boone very deliberately saddled, mounted, and rode away, heavily armed.

The wounded man lingered a week before he died.

Wallace had been a very popular man by reason of his frank, generous nature, his fearlessness, and an unusual capacity for friendship. His cowardly murder aroused the inhabitants of Young County to a white heat of indignation. The other Marlows were flung into prison on the charge of being accessory to the crime, an allegation they insistently denied. The countryside was scoured for Boone. A reward of $1,700 was offered for his capture, part of it by the state of Texas.

Posses rode far and wide. Boone dodged home at night and found a hiding place in a large straw stack into which he tunnelled. Here he stayed, revolvers strapped about his waist and rifle beside him, until the first ardour of the hunt was past. Under cover of darkness food was brought to him by the women. Meanwhile, Eugene Logan, a constable, and Sheriff Moore of Jack County found young Marlow's exhausted horse many miles from the scene of the killing. It did not occur to any of his hunters that he was snugly holed up so close to Graham.

It must have seemed to the other Marlows, locked up as they were in a steel cage of the Graham prison, that they were in a dangerous plight. Generally regarded as outlaws and rustlers, they realized that the wanton killing of Wallace had aroused public sentiment against them. According to the story they told afterward, the big cattle interests were feeding the flame of this resentment.

They decided to try to escape. From another prisoner named Speer, who occupied the cell opposite, they obtained a large pocket knife which he had secreted from the jailers when he had been searched. On the end of an old broom handle he passed this weapon across to George Marlow.

Each night, from dark till dawn, the brothers took turn about cutting a hole through the sheet of iron. It was slow work, but they were desperate, determined men. The refuse from their labour they hid under one of the beds to conceal it from the guards. At the end of a week the job was done.

The Marlows made a mistake. They were in too big a hurry.

Sheriff Collier and his deputy slept in the jail, but on the evening in question the officers were downtown. Instead of waiting until they had returned and gone to sleep the Marlows put their plan into execution at once. They tore their blankets into strips and made a rope. One end of this they tied to the timbers of the room. One after another they slid to the ground. A prisoner named Cummings escaped with them.

The refugees had no alternative except to strike for the Denson farm where their families were living. Here they would find food, warmer clothing, horses, and weapons. Cummings separated from the others. To avoid detection they took a roundabout way home. It was a bitterly cold night about the middle of January. The Marlows suffered intensely from the icy blasts that swept the plains. Day broke before they reached the farm. They could see the smoke of the newly lighted fires as they hurried forward.

From a neck of woods the fugitives crept toward

the house. At this moment Collier swept on them at the head of a posse and called upon them to surrender. It was a bitter, heartbreaking finale after all their labour and suffering. But there was no chance of escape. A dozen Winchesters and Colts covered them. The recaptured prisoners were marched back to Graham while their mother and their wives, unconscious of what had taken place, prepared and ate the breakfast their menfolks had almost reached the house in time to share.

What had occurred was simply what might have been expected. The Marlows had not allowed themselves a sufficient margin of time. They had missed liberty by five minutes, whereas if they had waited a few hours they might have been on the way to the Nation while the pursuit was still miles distant. The sheriff had returned to the jail, missed his prisoners, organized two posses (one to ride straight to the Denson farm and the other to follow the trail of the escaped men), and recaptured his prisoners.

The authorities took no more chances on the Marlows. They stopped at a blacksmith shop and shackled them together two and two. Charley and Alfred made one pair, George and Epp the other. So close a guard was kept on them that they had no possible chance to escape. The prison attendants were drawn from friends of the dead sheriff or from adherents of those opposed to the Marlows.

The four brothers were convinced their lives were in danger. They believed there was a conspiracy on the part of their enemies to accomplish their lynching.

This came out in the subsequent trials. The surviving Marlows charged that Sheriff Collier and Deputy United States Marshal Johnson repeatedly mentioned their fears that the Marlows would be taken from them and hanged by a mob. They named as other parties in the plot the county attorney P. A. Martin; a deputy constable, Eugene Logan; Morrison Wallace, nephew of the dead sheriff; Ben Williams, son of the county judge; Sam Waggoner, a constable; and Bruce Wheeler, Pink Brooks, Sam Cresswell, Clint Rutherford, Frank Harmison, Dick Cook, John Leavels, and Mill Hallice. All of these men, according to the Marlows, were close to the clique of cattlemen which had obtained legal control of the county machinery, and they did not intend that a "gang of rustlers" should escape the penalty for the murder of Wallace.

I do not say that such a conspiracy existed on the part of the officers, or that all of these men were in with the lawless element which proceeded to take things into its own hands. This was the contention of the Marlows. There is evidence to contravert the claim. For one thing, the number of officers on hand tends to show that the sheriff was watching for mob action. Eugene Logan and Dick Cook, Leavels the jailer, Collier, and his deputy, all slept at the jail. Yet the facts do not dovetail with any assurance that all these men were innocent of what followed. It is certain that some of them were involved.

On the night of January 17, 1889, not long before

daybreak, a party of about forty men surrounded the jail. Collier and his deputy Waggoner were absent, out of town on official business. Turnkey Leavels parleyed with the leader of the mob, but under compulsion of levelled guns opened the jail door. The other guards were captured while still asleep. Leavels was forced to call all of the prisoners except the Marlows out of the building, but as Speer passed he whispered to one of the doomed men:

"Look out, Charley. It's a mob."

The attackers were disguised by masks, but many of them were recognizable. They trooped upstairs and waited out of sight.

The turnkey (under the guns of the mob, he later said) opened the door of the cell where the Marlows were confined and called to one of them: "Man wants to see you, Charley."

Charley and Alf shuffled forward a few steps, as far as the door.

"Who wants me, Leavels?" asked Charley.

"Come out an' see."

"No, I reckon I'll stay here. If he wants me—well, he knows where I'm at."

Epp Marlow had been busy unscrewing a piece of water pipe. He handed it to Alf, the strongest of the brothers. The mob poured into the passage but stopped at sight of the prisoners quietly waiting for them.

"You've given us up to be killed like dogs," George accused Leavels bitterly.

"Leavels is doing only what he's got to do," one of the mob answered. "Come outa there, you-all. We want you."

It was a small cell, and the prisoners were known as desperate men. To bring them out alive might be a dangerous business. The leaders of the mob did not want to arouse the town by shooting, for this was an affair best kept dark. They hesitated.

One young fellow, Bob Hill by name, plunged forward. Charley Marlow caught him on the chin with a straight left. Hill was flung back, and his head struck the stone wall. He lay on the floor, groaning. Frank Harmison carried the bleeding lad down the stairs into the open.[1]

What followed was a curious exhibition of mob psychology. There were men in that masked crowd just as game as the Marlows. Harmison, for instance, was known to be both fearless and reckless. Others of those present were tough, hard-riding cattlemen of the border country. It is to be presumed they did not like the job they were on. A bad cause sometimes paralyzes courage. They had come there to lynch the Marlows. They were forty to four. The masked men were all armed. The four were not only without weapons, they were shackled. The mob leaders parleyed and blustered, but they could not bring themselves to attack. In the end they retired, bluffed out of their purpose.

---

[1]George Marlow related this incident about Bob Hill to me. He was very definite as to details. He said that young Hill died two days later from concussion of the brain. I have not been able to verify this. W. M. R.

All Young County talked of the affair next day. People could not understand why they had not shot down the prisoners when they made a stand for their lives. There was probably a mental inhibition. There is a fine line between the morality of shooting un-armed men and hanging them. The latter may be thought of as the execution of justice. The former bears the sinister aspect of murder. It may be a dis-tinction without a difference, but it is a very real one to those engaged in the unsavoury business of lynching.

Within two days Young County had something more thrilling to talk about. This time it was not a farce bordering on tragedy but red tragedy itself.

A wire was sent United States Marshal Cabell, then at Dallas, Texas, telling him of what had taken place. Cabell at once telephoned his deputy, Ed Johnson, to remove the Marlows to Weatherford for safekeeping.

Johnson selected as the guard Marion Wallace, Will Waggoner, Sam Cresswell, Will Hollis, P. A. Martin, and J. B. Girard. As soon as the Marlows saw their guard for the journey they protested. Sev-eral of these men, they claimed, had been among those who had tried to lynch them not forty-eight hours earlier.

"This is plain murder, Ed," George Marlow said.

He had cause for his apprehension. Night had al-ready fallen when the Marlows, with two other prisoners named Clift and Burkhardt, were put into a hack driven by George Martin. A man on horseback, lurking in the shadows, rode away as soon as the little cavalcade started. The deputy marshal and the other guards followed the prisoners in a buggy and another hack.

"What say we run a rope through their irons an' fasten them to the hack?" Cresswell suggested before they moved.

Johnson shook his head. "Not necessary," he said.

This decision of the deputy marshal saved the lives of several of the prisoners and cost those of several of their foes.

The vehicles moved slowly toward Dry Creek. On the far side of the creek was a long lane, separating two fields thick with mesquite. Down the sharp incline to the creek bed and up the opposite bank went the hacks.

George Marlow claimed afterward that just before the hacks crossed the creek Johnson came forward and said in a loud voice to his prisoners, "Boys, have a drink."

Charley spoke to his brothers. "That's a signal."

From the mesquite rose the figure of a man with a levelled rifle. "Halt. Throw up yore hands," he ordered.

The driver of the first hack slid from his seat and ran. Charley and Alf Marlow, chained together, rolled over the side of the hack and ran to the machine containing the guards. Alf wrenched a rifle from one of the posse and Charley jerked Johnson's revolver out of his hand. The other pair of brothers tumbled out of the hack as a man, carrying a rifle, rushed toward the crowd surrounding the second rig. George landed on the man's back and brought him to the ground. Epp pulled a revolver from his holster.

All this time there had been a good deal of firing. Johnson had been hit in the hand, either before or after he lost his revolver. The four brothers, now all armed, pushed toward each other. Alf dropped dead, shot through the brain. Epp went down, riddled by bullets.

The Marlows were famous shots. Bruce Wheeler, one of the attackers, was killed. Another of them, Eugene Logan, constable of the Belknap precinct, crept into the mesquite with a bullet in his thigh. Sam Cresswell, one of the guards, pitched forward dead. Another of the mob, shot in the breast and arm, was later carried to the Woods House at Graham, a very badly wounded man.

The prisoners, too, suffered heavily. In addition to the two dead Marlows, the other brothers were both wounded, Charley very severely. A load of buckshot had struck him in the breast, neck, and jaw. Clift had been shot in the thigh.

The mob had had enough. It fell back, panic-stricken, though only George Marlow remained on his feet to face it. He yelled a taunting defiance at the enemy.

One man heard that defiance and came back. The man was Frank Harmison, known as one of the gamest men in the county. He had been wounded early in the fight, but he was no quitter.

"Where you going?" one of his companions called.

"Going back to see it out," he called back scornfully.

He and George Marlow stood up, facing each other as though they had been fighting a set duel, and emptied revolvers at each other. Harmison fell dead, shot between the eyes.

The part played in this fight by the marshal's guard is a moot one. The Marlows claimed they were betrayed, that the guard offered no resistance and even supplied weapons to the mob, and that Cresswell was killed and Johnson wounded when they turned on their prisoners. The officers denied this and said they suffered defending the prisoners. The Graham *Leader* said a day or two later:

> The first shot hit Deputy Marshal Johnson in his only hand, thus disabling him. As soon as the firing commenced the Marlows rolled out of the hack and got to Mr. Johnson's hack, where they got hold of some arms and fired into the mob. It is thought the prisoners did more shooting than the guard. The mob became demoralized and the prisoners held the field.

The condition of the surviving Marlows was desperate. Bleeding from a dozen wounds, Charley could scarcely stand. Both he and George were chained to the bodies of the dead brothers. It was impossible for them to escape with such a weight dragging at their feet. The thing that had to be done was gruesome enough. With a knife found in Cresswell's pocket they disjointed the ankles of the men to whom they were chained and so freed themselves.

George gathered such arms and ammunition as he found scattered about the battlefield. He helped his brother into the hack that still stood there. Clift and Burkhardt joined them. They drove to Finis, and at a blacksmith shop had the chains knocked from their limbs. Here Burkhardt left them. The others drove to the Denson farm.

The wounds of the escaped prisoners were dressed. A man was sent to town for a doctor. Dr. Price rode out to the farm. With him went Sheriff Collier and a very large posse.

The house had been put into a state of defence, and those within served notice that they could not be taken without a fight. Dr. Price went inside and dressed the wounds of the three men. Charley was so badly wounded that it was thought he could not live. Clift had a ragged hole in his thigh. Both of them could still handle a gun, however. Dr. Price reported to the sheriffs (the sheriff of Jacks County had by this time arrived with a second posse) that the besieged men would surrender only to United States Marshal Cabell, that they were well armed, and that they would fight to the end.

It is said that Collier proposed to storm the place. The sheriff of Jacks declined to join him in this. It was his opinion that enough blood had been shed, and he was not sure that the law would justify him in view of what had occurred. Most of those present agreed with him.

Marion Lasater and Will Gilmore walked up to the cabin with a flag of truce and held parley with George Marlow. They entered the cabin and promised to send for Cabell. Two days later Cabell's deputy arrived from Dallas, and the wounded men surrendered.

They were taken to Dallas. In spite of predictions Charley stood the journey and reached the city alive. Slowly he recovered.

The Graham *Leader* came out flat-footed with a demand that the lawbreakers who had attacked the prisoners be convicted and punished. It had no lance to break for the Marlows. The paper commented as follows:

It is said that when Epp Marlow was found he had a Winchester by his side and a pistol in his hand with all the chambers empty. They were a desperate set of men, and no doubt have been in many shooting scrapes, but that does not justify an armed mob in killing them. They were prisoners and as such entitled to the protection of the law. . . . The law-abiding citizens of the county demand that the proper authorities use every means to bring these violators of the law to trial. They should not be allowed to go unpunished.

A week later three men drove up to the office of Sheriff Collier. They gave their names as Beavers, Harbolt, and Direkson. They said they lived in the Chickasaw Nation and invited the sheriff to come out and see what they had with them. In the wagon outside was the body of Boone Marlow. An inquest was held by Squire Starrett. The men testified that they had killed the outlaw on Hell Creek, Comanche Nation, twenty miles east of Fort Sill, while he was resisting arrest. The authorities were satisfied, and the reward was paid the men.

Two months later these three men were indicted for the murder of Boone Marlow. It was claimed that they had poisoned him, that they had wanted the reward but had lacked the courage to arrest him alive. "It is a curious fact," comments the *Leader*, "that everybody who has anything to do with the Marlows has more or less trouble over them."

The mob leaders were having a good deal of trouble. At the ensuing election in Young County the issue was mob or anti-mob. Marion Lasater was candidate for sheriff on the side of the law enforcement party. He was elected. Wholesale indictments were brought against the lynchers.

The Federal government took up the matter. Most of the survivors named in this story were summoned to appear before a grand jury at Dallas. Martin, Waggoner, Leavels, Logan, and Cook, who had all been officials at the time of the trouble, were arrested on the charge of opposing and obstructing a deputy United States marshal in the discharge of his duty. Marion and Ed Wallace, Pink Brooks, W. R. Benedict, and Verner Wilkerson were also taken into custody; the first four on the charge already named, the fifth for murder and conspiracy to murder. There were other indictments. The court changed the venue of the local cases to Jack County on account of the state of public sentiment. Meanwhile, George and Charley Marlow were held under guard, both as witnesses in the cases named and as defendants in two horse-theft charges.

The cases dragged on for years. Only three convictions were obtained, and these were against Eugene Logan, Sam Waggoner, and Marion Wallace. None of them ever served any part of their sentence. The

Marlows were not convicted in the rustling cases filed against them.

In the end Young County decided it was best to forget the whole bad business, to wipe the slate clean and begin again. The days when the quiet little town of Graham was a slaughter house because of men's lawless passions are now only a fading memory in the minds of a few old-timers.

THE ESTANCIA LAND GRANTS

*The Story of Romance and Tragedy That Cen-
tred About the Struggle for the Possession of a
Vast and Noble Domain in the Southwest*

IN THE story of the Southwest nothing is more interesting and dramatic than the history of the great
land grants made to privileged individuals by the
Spanish crown and later by the Mexican government.
They involved, or have involved, immense interests.
The contests for these claims have made men bankrupt by scores, have deprived thousands of settlers of
their homes, have created widespread uncertainty
regarding the legal ownership of land, retarding, on
account of this unrest, the development of the country, and have, in more than one instance, splashed
with blood the adobe walls of historic haciendas.

Attempting as they did to establish in Colorado,
California, New Mexico, and Arizona, even as late
as the middle decades of the Nineteenth Century, a
semi-feudal system, splendid in its proportions, the
experiment failed only because the times were over-
ripe for the endurance of the old monarchial tradi-
tions. Nevertheless, the attempt was a magnificent
one. It brought with it to the New World all the glam-
our and romance of the vanishing race of cavaliers

of Castile. It laid the foundations of a new colonial empire brilliant in conception, destined to fail only because the advancing tide of our restless Western democracy was already lapping at its outer walls.

The final determination of these great land grants has been diverse, and the issue has depended frequently upon apparently trivial accidents. Take, for example, the Las Animas grant of more than four million acres in southeastern Colorado. This grant, made by Governor Manuel Armijo in 1843 to Cornelio Vigil and Ceran St. Vrain, was rejected because St. Vrain, in support of his claim, offered to the Senate Committee in 1860 a rough map of the tract claimed by him. This map showed all too clearly that the grant exceeded twenty times the eleven square leagues allowed by the Mexican law of 1824 and 1828 to be granted in a single block. But for this map St. Vrain's claim would probably have passed the Senate Committee almost unnoticed, as a score of others had done, and his title made good to a territory larger than some states, and including the present counties in Colorado of Huerfano, Las Animas, and Otero, as well as parts of Bent and Pueblo, together with a score of cities, towns, and villages since located in that territory.

The famous Maxwell grant in New Mexico was ratified by Congress, but the conflicting Estancia grants, also in New Mexico, were rejected by the Court of Claims and have recently been thrown open to settlement for homesteaders by the government. Already the rich valley and the wooded hills where the great herds of the Spanish grandees roamed have been crossed by the Santa Fe Central and brought into touch with the market. The springs for which Manuel B. Otero, one of the most promising young Spaniards in the territory, fought and died at the old ranch house, are to be converted into a summer resort. *Tempora mutantur!*

The history of the Estancia land grant and the struggle of rival claimants is a peculiarly interesting one, involving the more notable of the rich, blue-blooded Spanish families of New Mexico and the romantic life story of the most beautiful daughter of Castile in that territory. Between the lines of yellow Spanish documents and the legal verbiage of its musty law records one may read the throb of youthful passion, of high-pulsed hope, and of radiating romance. Some of the actors in that drama have died to the sound of cracking revolvers, some have passed away in the ripeness of age, others are still full of lusty life. But the old era of prodigal Spanish hospitality and magnificence has slipped away forever into the seven thousand years of yesterday.

Don Bartolomé Baca, the original grantee of the princely Estancia estate of nearly a million and a half acres of valuable land, was a lineal descendent of an ancient noble family in Spain. In the New World he was a man notable as a soldier, a ruler, and a grandee. Possessed of very great wealth, he was generous and public spirited even beyond the wont of his class. On several occasions, when the people in the province suffered from the raids of the Indians, he distributed thousands of his sheep to relieve their needs. These were furnished ostensibly as a loan, but he never asked for their return.

It is recorded that when in 1870 Don Bartolomé Baca, then a very old man, came to die, he sent for his friend and secretary, Francisco de Maradiaga, a learned priest prominent in the territory. Baca had large sums of money loaned all over New Mexico and held hundreds of mortgages from the people who owed him. In the presence of his children the old Don dictated his will, distributing his property with minute attention to detail. But of his numerous mortgages he said not a word. One of his sons asked him why he did not say which of his children was to inherit these. He replied that he would presently dispose of them, and having concluded his other affairs he had the priest Maradiaga burn the mortgages in his presence in the great fireplace set in the adobe chamber. There were then no official records kept of such papers, so that their destruction was irrevocable. Thus Baca, even to his death, looked out for the welfare of the poor peons indebted to him.

Yet despite his generosity and his munificence, Baca was an able man and flourished greatly. His flocks and herds spread over a score of hills and valleys until they numbered several hundred thousand.

While living in Casa, Colorado, in the then county of Valencia, he asked of Facundo Megares, governor of the royal province of New Mexico, then pertaining to the crown of Spain, a grant of land on which to pasture his sheep and cattle. Baca had already started a little town in the mountains and named it Torreon (tower). Here he had built a tower house that overlooked the valley so that he might be able to protect himself and his dependents from the sudden attacks of Indians.

Just as in the old feudal days the king used to hold the country by means of grants to powerful barons, so the representatives of Spain were empowered to hold its royal provinces in the New World against Indians and other possible claimants by the assistance of the great proprietors.

Governor Megares ordered the constitutional alcalde José Garcia de la Mora to execute the act for possession to Baca of a certain tract of land bounded on the south by Crow Springs (Ojo del Cuervo), following its *cordillera* to the Salt Springs (Ojo del Chico), on the east by the Pedornal Mountains (Cerro de Pedornal), on the north by the Buffalo Spring (Ojo del Cibolo), and on the west by the summit of the mountain (la altura de la Cierra). This the alcalde did, and Baca formally took possession on July 2, 1819. On the occasion when he occupied the land with his cattle, sheep, and horses, Jesus Salvedra, Antonio Marquez, and other peons were present. No survey of the land was made, but the grant was estimated to contain about a million and a half acres, or nearly twenty-five hundred square miles.

Until the time of his death Don Bartolomé Baca grazed his herds over this great tract, larger than the state of Delaware; and at times cultivated some of it.

He visited his estate occasionally, but does not seem, at any time, to have taken up his permanent residence there. The peculiarity of this grant is that it appears to have been a grazing rather than an agricultural one, since the latter would have necessitated a four-years' residence on the part of the grantee. According to the decision of the surveyor general many years later, a decision adverse to the Baca claim, no record of an actual grant has been shown, although the acting governor certainly ordered the transfer of land. This he adjudged to be an imperfect title.

Another point that militated against the Baca claim was that subsequent grants were made of lands included in this grant, both within the lifetime of the original grantee and after his death, without protest on the part of Baca or his heirs. Indeed Don Bartolomé Baca succeeded Megares as governor and captain general of the province of New Mexico, and, while he was President of the Ayuntamiento, or Council at Tome, even officially indorsed grants of land included in the Baca Estancia estate. One of these grants was to a colony of farmers at Manzana, and was situated right in the heart of the Baca estate. This grant was made with the concurrence of Don Bartolomé on September 22, 1829. The grants of Ojo del Medio in November, 1831, and of Tejique in March, 1834, were also made with the knowledge of Baca. Therefore the United States Court of Private Land Claims years later adjudged that Baca had abandoned his grant, and the Supreme Court of the

United States sustained this view. The Baca heirs have always denied this, alleging that the generous old Don was willing to have these small grants made to develop the country, to help settlers, as well as to supply men to assist him in protecting his herds and flocks from the Indians.

Meanwhile, Mexico became a country independent of Spain. The last Mexican governor of the province of New Mexico, Manuel Armijo, was granted by the President of the country extraordinary powers for the disposition of lands on account of having been victorious in a battle with Texas Rangers attempting to assert the independence of that territory. Out of the very heart of the Baca grant he carved a piece of nearly half a million acres, including both the Antelope and the Estancia springs as well as others south of them, and conveyed it on December 7, 1845, to Antonio Sandoval, for "services to the government of Mexico." The latter, a roving Spanish soldier, deeded it to Gervacio Nolan, from whose heirs Joel P. Whitney, a Boston capitalist, purchased in 1878 the grant, at the time believing the title to be perfect. The Boston millionaire sent his brother, James G. Whitney, out to take charge of his estate in New Mexico, near which district ranged about 25,000 cattle owned him by. Thus another powerful claimant for the land about Estancia was created by Armijo's ill-considered grant.

In 1874 Don Manuel Antonio Otero, together with his brother, the Hon. Miguel Antonio Otero, father of a recent governor of New Mexico, and himself later both governor and delegate to Congress, bought from the Baca heirs in the city of Mexico all their interests in the Don Bartolomé Baca Estancia land grant. In 1881 Don Manuel Antonio Otero died and his only son, Manuel B. Otero, took charge of the estate, on which he was running about 35,000 sheep.

Manuel B. Otero was a typical Otero. A handsome young blond of splendid physique, he had inherited the strict integrity of his father and uncle, as well as their uncurbed pride of blood. He was the product of a German university, and upon his return to this country he had married Eloisa Luna, the most beautiful girl in the territory, then about sixteen years old, and just returned from a New York convent where she had been educated. The daughter of the Hon. Antonio José Luna and of Doña Isabel Baca y Castillo, Eloisa was the direct descendant of one of the greatest characters in Spanish history, Don Alvaro de Luna, who lost his head on account of a misunderstanding with the King. About the year 1695, after the death of Don Alvaro, the Lunas came to the royal province of New Mexico. One of them, the Duke of Albuquerque, founded the town of that name, and his cousin, the Count de Luna, built the neighbouring village of Los Lunas as a focal point for his retainers to congregate.

It was inevitable that there should be in time a clash between the vaqueros of Whitney and the herders of Otero. There was first the old antipathy between sheep and cattle, intensified in this case because of racial differences. In addition to this their masters were rival claimants for this rich grazing ground, one especially well adapted both to cattle and sheep. Trouble between the Whitney and the Otero peons broke out occasionally, but simmered without coming to a head.

There were about two hundred squatters on the Estancia grants, and against one of these, named McAfee, Whitney brought a test case and was granted judgment by the territorial Supreme Court. James G. Whitney and his vaqueros rode to the Barendo or Antelope Springs, where the McAfee ranch was located, to dispossess the squatter. An arrangement was made with McAfee whereby Whitney bought his cattle and improvements from him at a good price, the squatter relinquishing his right of appeal to the United States Supreme Court.

The decision in the case of the squatter McAfee had no application to the Baca claim. A suit was pending in the courts between Otero and Whitney, the representatives of the original Baca and Sandoval grants, but Whitney, instead of waiting to abide the decision of the court, proceeded to treat Otero as a squatter and rode to the adobe ranch house at Estancia to dispossess Otero's major-domo, Jesus M. Chaves. Fearing trouble, he and his party went armed. With him and his vaqueros were his brother-in-law, Alexander Fernandez, a nephew named Haines, and a young man named Arthur Bailhache. He had already served a peremptory notice to Otero to vacate before Thursday, which order young Otero had refused to obey. The party took possession of the little ranch house and sat up all night playing cards in high spirits.

Jesus Chaves, the major-domo, hearing that the Whitney party was on the way to the ranch, had sent a messenger to Manuel B. Otero's home at La Constancia, where he was staying with his beautiful young wife and two children. With his brother-in-law, Carlos Armijo, and a vaquero or two, Otero started at once for the scene of trouble, leaving word for another brother-in-law, Dr. Edward C. Henriques, to follow as soon as he could. The latter, with several attendants, caught up with the Otero party just before it reached the Estancia adobe house. Both parties had travelled all night in their haste.

The meeting between Otero and Whitney was distant. The young Mexican was courteous but stern, the American not disposed to yield what he thought to be his rights.

"Have you a writ of ejectment, sir?" Otero asked of Whitney, after they had broached the business of the day.

"I have, but not with me," replied the Bostonian.

"Then you are proceeding contrary to law."

"Not at all," replied the American, "you, as a squatter, are outside the law. I order you to vacate the premises."

"And I decline," replied Otero. "I am no squatter."

The issue had come quickly. There was a hot word or two, a threat, and several revolvers were quietly loosened in their scabbards. Henriques, according to the testimony of the Whitney faction, was especially belligerent. Whitney later testified that he heard a gun click behind him and immediately drew his pistol.

"Drop that gun," cried Henriques to Whitney, covering him from behind.

The American closed with him, and in the scuffle both their revolvers were discharged. Somebody whipped up a gun and fired at Otero. There was another shot and Alexander Fernandez rolled under the bed on which he had been sitting, with a bullet in his heart. A fusillade followed. Bailhache, unarmed, dropped to the floor, and Armijo, also without a weapon, bolted through the door.

When the smoke cleared away the place looked like a shambles. Otero was seen staggering to the door, clutching at his neck from which the blood was spurting in jets. Whitney, with eleven bullets in him, lay on the floor writhing in agony. Fernandez had expired, and Dr. Henriques was stretched across a cot with two bullets in his arm, one of which had severed an artery at the wrist. His revolver was still pointed at Whitney.

"For God's sake, don't shoot," cried the latter.

Henriques flung his gun away.

The Otero forces took possession of the ranch house. Brown, Whitney's cook, ran in and was disarmed.

"You had better attend to your master," said Henriques.

Otero was removed to another room, but died before sunset. A crowd gathered, murmuring threats against Whitney. He was removed secretly and taken in a wagon to Las Vegas. On arriving there he was arrested by two deputy sheriffs, Page B. Otero, and his brother, afterward governor. An order was issued by the court to take him to Los Lunas for a preliminary examination, but on the arrival of the train at Albuquerque he was released on a writ of habeas corpus. He was subsequently tried and acquitted. He lived nearly twenty years, but never recovered fully from his terrible experience.

A few years after the tragedy there drifted into the Southwest a young Italian, Alfred M. Bergère by name, a man handsome, cultured, and distinguished to a degree even beside the courtly and aristocratic Spaniards of New Mexico. He was of pure Italian blood, though born in England and educated at Queen's College. He fell in love at sight with the young widow of Manuel B. Otero and wooed her with all the ardour of the Latin races. From a host of admirers he won her, and became henceforth an indomitable champion of his wife's rights as represented by the Baca grant. He bought out the other heirs and championed her case from court to court at an expense of a quarter million dollars.

He was hampered by lack of the original grant papers. As it chanced a grandson of old Bartolomé Baca, while eating a Mexican cake at his home at Belen, New Mexico, noticed that the paper in which it had been cooked had his grandfather's name on it. An investigation showed that it was part of the original order of Governor Megares. In an old trunk the rest of the paper, with the exception of a little corner, was found and turned over to Bergère.

The court of private land claims at Santa Fe awarded to the Baca claimants eleven square leagues, this being all that could be given on a Mexican grant. But Bergère, because the original grant had been a Spanish and not a Mexican one, appealed on behalf of himself and his wife.

The case was tried at length before the Supreme Court of the United States, and the grant rejected on the grounds that after the final adjudication there was no proof that Governor Megares had signed the approval of the grant as required by law, since the missing corner of the approval containing part of his name had been destroyed.

As the Sandoval grant had already been rejected by the Court of Claims, all the territory contained in the famous Estancia grants reverted to the government and was thrown open for homestead entry. It is pleasant to be able to record that Mr. Bergère, though he lost his fight on behalf of his wife for a great fortune, owned by homestead entry for himself and family the best parts of the Estancia estate, those on which the famous springs are situated and which are most suitable for irrigation out of many arable farms that have since been taken up by eager home seekers.

Alfred M. Bergère still lives at Santa Fe. Some years ago I visited his home, a typical Spanish house of the better class. His wife, formerly Eloisa Luna, was the mother of eleven dark-eyed handsome children. So young she looked that she might have been the eldest sister of that interesting family. The courts had decreed that she was no longer Princess of Estancia, but with old Castilian grace she was queening it over a happy American home where old family heirlooms still reminded the fortunate guest of the days when Dons and Doñas ruled magnificently the Southwest under royal grant from Spain.

A FORGOTTEN FILIBUSTER

The Story of How Less Than One Hundred Americans Set Out to Conquer a Great Nation Under the Leadership of That Picturesque Fire Eater Henry A. Crabbe

DURING the twenty-five years just prior to the Civil War, the filibuster found in this country a soil peculiarly fertile for the propagation of his restless and ambitious ideas. The institution of slavery was fighting for existence, and the hotheads of the South were seeking to obtain power by expanding the territory where their cherished doctrine obtained. For this reason Texas, Cuba, Mexico, and Nicaragua became coveted prizes for the adventurous sons of Dixie.

No tales of border romance contain more thrilling adventure than the simple record of these land buccaneers, who set out like the sea rovers of old to carve their fortunes from the gathered treasures and domains of the Spanish race. One may often question their motive, but one may nearly always find in them a spirit of gallantry and devotion worthy of a better cause than the forlorn hope which sent them on their reckless way to death. And surely many of them—instance Travis, Crockett, and Cameron—were true patriots as well as filibusters. Around the brave lives and heroic deaths of these men, as well as Bowie, Crittenden, Henningsen, Crabbe, Walker, and a thousand of their forgotten comrades, the romance of the ante-bellum days clusters. They were filibusters by the written law of nations, and they paid for their devoted folly by dying with the sword in their hands or with their backs to the wall, at the hands of Spanish marksmen.

The line between the filibuster and the patriot is one not easily drawn. Houston and Bolivar are national heroes because they succeeded; Walker and De Boulbon are remembered as filibusters because they failed. This is the verdict of history, and from it there is no appeal. But whatever their motive, whether success or the grave awaited them—and it was nearly always the latter—their story is inspiring.

Barrett Travis, the young commander of the Alamo, kept the flag flying against five thousand Mexicans until his own hundred and seventy-five men had been cut down to a man. He was fighting the battle of freedom. Nevertheless, he was a filibuster.

So, technically, was the boy Kentuckian George B. Crittenden, who was captured with his comrades of the Mier expedition. The order was given that the party be decimated. Crittenden drew a white bean and was safe. But he gave it to a comrade.

"You have a wife and children, but I have none. I can take another chance," he said.

He was fortunate enough to draw another white bean and lived to fight in both the Mexican and the

Civil wars, reaching the rank of brigadier-general on the Confederate side, in the latter.

Some years later his cousin, Col. W. S. Crittenden, a veteran of the Mexican War, though only twenty-eight years old, lost his life while filibustering in Cuba. After he was captured the order came for his execution. He stood against a wall at Havana with head up and unflinching eyes. They ordered him to kneel, but he declined. "An American kneels only to God," he said, and next instant he fell forward on his face riddled with bullets.

These incidents may be paralleled by a hundred others as dramatic. It was a time when the romance of the South was seeking a vent for its energy. Texas became the first field for these restless chivalrous spirits, and California, the magic land of gold, was a magnet to the later ones. From the Golden Gate the expeditions of Count Gaston de Raoussett-Boulbon, William Walker, and Henry A. Crabbe set out at different times to carve an empire from Mexican territory with their swords. It was in April, 1857, while Walker was fighting for his life in Nicaragua, that the Crabbe tragedy occurred at Cavorca in the province of Sonora.

Crabbe was a native of Mississippi. Like hundreds of other adventurous spirits he had been attracted to California by the gold discoveries. By virtue of natural fitness, he was a born leader. A man of determined bravery and of uncommon ability, more than six feet in height and strongly built, handsome and magnetic, he was a man to win and hold friends.

With much of the Southern charm of manner about him, he was as gentle and as generous as he was gallant. He had, however, more than a touch of instability and of uncurbed pride to hamper his inordinate ambition.

By marrying into the Ainsa family, he had become connected with Mexico. Ainsa himself was a prominent citizen of Sonora, who had come to California at the time of the gold rush. He was of Spanish and Filipino extraction, but was very prominent in the political affairs of his adopted state. His attractive, well-educated sons and daughters held a high place socially. The marriage of Augustin Ainsa, one of the sons, drew Crabbe to Mexico in March, 1856.

Sonora was at this time unknown to eastern Mexicans. From 1856 to 1877 Mexico was passing through a period of civil and foreign wars, and it was during this time that the character of the province of Sonora was formed. The power of the central government of Mexico over the province was tenuous in the extreme. Previous to 1856 there had been several governors who had established themselves as dictators in fact, until the turn of the wheel of fortune had flung them into exile. Governor José de Aguilar was one of these. He went into retirement on account of a threatened revolution, and in his place Ignacio Pesqueira came rapidly to the front. In 1856 Pesqueira was a man of some note, being president of the council of state. He was a man of great ability, destined for two decades to be the dictator of Sonora.

The social discontent then existing in that province

appealed greatly to Crabbe's instinct for practical politics. General Gandara had just been legally elected governor of Sonora, but he was neither popular nor capable. He used his position to enrich himself, and by so doing imposed heavy taxes and great hardships upon a people already poverty-stricken. The sources of national revenue were farmed out to English and American contractors. This resulted in extortionate monopolies and in financial depression, but though petitioned to remedy this, Gandara paid no heed, even though the petitioners were among the leading citizens of the state. To Crabbe it was at once plain that a revolution was ripening.

The party of the opposition made so much of Crabbe that Gandara grew suspicious of his presence. He saw the Californian wined and dined so extensively by Pesqueira, Aguilar, and Rodriguez, the leaders of the party opposed to him, that it took no diviner to guess that they were soliciting the help of the American to carry through a revolution. A good pretext for their fêting of Crabbe was found in the circumstance that he had years before defeated a hostile band of Apaches just returning from a bloody raid into Sonora, and had saved the captive women and children the savages had with them.

Not feeling himself strong enough to crush his enemies openly, Gandara wrote to the city of Mexico for help. But before a reply reached him, Crabbe had returned to California. He had entered into an agreement with the Pesqueira faction, the terms of which were in substance that Crabbe should lead down into Sonora a thousand Americans to make certain the success of a revolution to be started by Pesqueira and his followers. The latter were to begin the revolution in order to give the movement a popular and patriotic character. Crabbe's reward was to be a wide strip of territory along the northern frontier, to be granted under the pretext that the American "colonists" were to receive it for protecting Sonora from the Apaches.

It is characteristic of Crabbe that he dallied with his golden chance until it was gone. Returning to California, his lack of unity of purpose caused him to delay. The politics of California had grown suddenly vitally interesting to him. Politically, he had been a Whig dyed in the wool. He was one of the most popular men in California. An acknowledged leader in the state senate, he joined in 1855 the Knownothing party, which was the political heir of the defunct Whig faction. He became at once a leading candidate for the seat in the United States Senate left vacant by the retirement of Dr. Gwin. Among the other prominent candidates were ex-Senator Henry S. Foote of Mississippi and Col. Edward C. Marshall, a former representative in Congress from California. The state legislature could not agree as to a senator and failed to elect. Crabbe's restless energy, curbed in this direction, flung itself anew into the Sonora filibustering expedition.

But he was too late. Ignacio Pesqueira's wily plotting had already borne issue. Alienating a portion of the Yaqui Indians from Gandara and calling upon all the discontented elements to rally to his banner, he defeated Gandara and drove him across the border. Next year (though that is another story) Pesqueira again defeated his rival in a decisive battle at Bacanora on February 24, 1858. In this battle Gandara was slain.

Crabbe meanwhile, not being himself a trained soldier, is believed to have entered into an agreement with Gen. John G. Cosby who had commanded in the Rogue River Indian War of 1855-1856, by which the latter was to coöperate with him and take charge of raising the troops. There were at the time thousands of dare-devils in California, thrown out of employment by the playing out of the placer diggings, who would have jumped at the chance of joining such an expedition. But Cosby preferred to furnish them from his own soldiers. Crabbe had, however, reserved the right to choose a company of his own friends. Among those who joined Crabbe were John Henry, Col. R. Nat Wood, ex-Senator McCoun, Captain McKinney, Judge Shafer, Major Robert Wood, Major Tozier, Dr. Evans, and Dr. Oxley. Many of them were men who had been prominent in the affairs of California and Arizona, though some of them had, no doubt, outlived their popularity, or were ready to seek a short cut to fortune. Seven former members of the legislature, a state senator, a former state treasurer and state comptroller, were among those who joined Crabbe. Hundreds of them were eager to enlist, but were refused because Crabbe was apparently relying on the promise of General Cosby.

Crabbe had promised Pesqueira that there would be no delay, but Pesqueira had been forced to make his great coup alone. Still Crabbe dallied, waiting for the promised succours.

His friend Walker had already won Nicaragua and gained control of the isthmus transit route, then a matter of the first importance to the steamship lines of San Francisco. Walker needed men greatly. He knew Crabbe well and wanted the thousand men he was about to raise. So he offered Crabbe five hundred dollars a month, agreeing to pay in advance for two years, and to find him free passage for himself and his family to New Orleans if he would join the great filibuster. Crabbe was pressed by his friends to accept this offer. He needed money badly and the Sonora project was hazardous. But the vision of leadership and his promise to Pesqueira outweighed the allurements of the Nicaragua offer.

On January 21, 1857, the steamer *Sea Bird* put out from the harbour of San Francisco with seventy filibusters on board. They called themselves the American and Arizona Mining and Emigration Company, though it was well known for what purpose they went. On the 24th, the steamer reached San Pedro. At El Monte, not far from Los Angeles, the party outfitted and accepted a few fresh recruits.

Never a company of adventurers went to death more blithely than this little band. Most of them were young men under twenty-five, and they wooed adventure like a mistress. They relied on Crabbe's contract with Pesqueira and the succours which were to be sent them later from San Francisco. As the affair eventuated both of these hopes were destined to prove futile, but it is not at all certain that even if they had known beforehand that Pesqueira and Cosby would both fail them, they would not still have attempted the adventure.

Pushing into the desert, the ninety men reached Yuma on February 27th. A small party under the command of Col. Robert Wood and Major Tozier was here detailed to go up the Gila River and secure reinforcements if possible. On March 4th, Crabbe and the rest of his men left Yuma, marching directly across the Colorado desert toward Sonoita, Arizona. They camped one night at a place still known as Filibuster's Camp. They reached Sonoita late in the evening of March 25th. Here was located the American trading post of Belknap and Dunbar, at which Jesus Ainsa was employed. Ainsa endeavoured to dissuade his brother-in-law from carrying out his mad enterprise, but as Charles D. Poston puts it, both Crabbe and his men were "hell-bent on going."

The filibusters appear to have been intoxicated with the lust of gain, for they are said to have robbed right and left as they advanced. From mission churches they snatched golden images and the embroidered altar cloths. The sight of this looting roused the natives to fury and their subsequent treatment of the filibusters has been excused because of this shameful despoliation. The treasure filched by the filibusters was subsequently buried by them.

Leaving Captain McKinney with twenty men at Cabeza Prieta to gather horses and provisions, the main body pushed eagerly forward. They had been told by a Papago Indian that a large vessel laden with men had just landed on the coast. They supposed this to be the expected reinforcements and were made the keener to carry the day before the arrival of their friends. Cosby, however, had not moved at all in the matter, and on this account friends of Crabbe had dispatched men to ride night and day to stop him before he went too far. These riders were too late and reached Fort Yuma only in time to hear of the fate of the party. James O'Meara, sometime editor of the San Francisco *Examiner*, lays the blame of the Crabbe massacre upon General Cosby and the monopolist merchants at Guaymas, who were in the employ of San Francisco capitalists. This combination controlled the rich mines and the commerce of Sonora. They knew that the thousand men Crabbe expected from San Francisco would never arrive, but they let him go to his fate without warning. The success of Crabbe would have meant the opening of this territory to rival companies. Therefore, without compunction they let him sacrifice himself. According to O'Meara, Cosby never set foot again in Sacramento, where Crabbe had hundreds of friends. He began at once to live in affluence and at a fast pace. The inference is that he had been bought by Crabbe's opponents. This charge, it is only fair to say, has never been proved. He was killed while driving soon afterward.

On crossing the border, Crabbe issued a statement to the effect that he had come on a peaceable errand of colonization. But this deceived nobody, and José Maria Redondo, prefect of the department of Altar, made immediate preparations to check the invaders. He notified Pesqueira, and the latter, having achieved his ambition and not caring to offend the natives by showing that he was in alliance with the hated "Americanos," repudiated his secret compact with Crabbe by ordering Lieutenant Gabilondo to attack him. So by treachery he avoided the stigma of disloyalty that recognition of Crabbe would have cast upon him.

But Crabbe had too much placed on this throw to give up without a fight. Much time and money were involved in his expedition, and he relied on the help of his friends in Sonora to start a native outbreak. Perhaps he had visions of displacing Pesqueira.

Crabbe had forwarded a letter to Redondo as soon as he discovered that he was to be met with arms. He reiterated his peaceable intent, though admitting in the same sentence that nine hundred men were on their way to join him. He accused the Mexicans of poisoning the wells and instigating the Papagos against him and his men. His letter concluded with a threat:

But have a care, sir, for whatever we may be caused to suffer shall return upon the heads of you and of those who assist you! I had never considered it possible that you would have defiled yourselves by resorting to such barbarous practices. I have come to your country because I have a right to follow the maxims of civilization. I have come, as I have amply proved, with the expectation of being received with open arms; but now I believe that I am to find my death among an enemy destitute of humanity. But, as against my companions now here, and those who are to arrive, I protest against any wrong step. Finally, you must reflect; bear this in mind: if blood is shed, on your hands be it and not on mine. Nevertheless, you can assure yourself and continue with your hostile preparations; for, as for me, I shall at once proceed to where I have intended to go for some time, and am ready to start. I am the leader, and my purpose is to act in accordance with the natural law of self-preservation. Until we meet at Altar, I remain

Your ob'dt serv't,
HENRY A. CRABBE.

This letter was forwarded to Pesqueira. The treacherous governor replied to it by issuing a proclamation to his people:

Free Sonorians, to arms, all!

Now has sounded the hour I recently announced, in which you must prepare for the bloody struggle you are about to enter into.

Let us fly, then, to chastise, with all the fury that can scarcely be contained in a heart swelling with resentment against coercion, the savage filibuster who has dared, in unhappy hour! to tread our nation's soil, and to arouse, insensate! our wrath.

Nothing of mercy, nothing of generous sentiments for this *canaille !*

Let it die like a wild beast, which, trampling upon the rights of men and scorning every law and institution of society, dares invoke the law of nature as its only guide, and to call upon brute force as its chosen ally.

Sonorians! Let our reconciliation be made sincere by a common hatred for this cursed horde of pirates, without country, without religion, without honour. Let the only mark to distinguish us and to protect our foreheads, not only against hostile bullets, but also against humiliation and insult, be the tricoloured ribbon, sublime creation of the genius of Iguala.

Upon it let there be written the grand words "*Liberty or Death*," and henceforth shall it bear for us one more significance—the powerful, invincible union of the two parties which have lately divided our state in civil war. We shall soon return all loaded with glory, after having forever secured the prosperity of Sonora, and established, in defiance of tyranny, this principle, *The people that wants to be free, will be so.* Meanwhile, citizens, relieve your hearts by giving free course to the enthusiasm which now burdens them.

Live Mexico! Death to the Filibusters!
March 30, 1857.

Certainly patriotism is the last resort of scoundrels.

The filibusters pushed on toward Cavorca. Early in the morning of April 1st a party of Mexicans in ambush fired a volley upon them, just as a strong force under Colonel Rodriguez was discovered drawn up in front to oppose the way. The Americans fired a volley and dashed forward, driving the natives pell-mell before them. Colonel Rodriguez was killed while exhorting his men to stand their ground.

Lieutenant Gabilondo rallied his men in the plaza of the little town of Cavorca, fortifying the church and taking possession of it. Meanwhile, the Crabbe party, flushed with victory, rode through fields of young wheat to the plaza. Along a narrow Mexican street they galloped under a heavy cross-fire from soldiers concealed in the houses, to the open square beyond. Gabilondo's deadly fire drove them into the adobe huts opposite the church. A constant fusillade was poured upon the Americans from all sides, as the natives had taken courage upon discovering the smallness of their force.

Even before reaching cover the Crabbe party had

suffered severely. "Clock" Small and a teamster called "Shorty" had been killed, and William Cheney, John George, and a lawyer named Clark, from El Monte, mortally wounded. A score of others suffered from wounds more or less severe.

The necessity of driving Gabilondo's force from the church which commanded their position, soon became apparent. As many of the party as were still able to move made a sortie against the church, but they were repulsed with considerable loss. Again that night, under cover of darkness, thirty of them sallied out in an attempt to surprise the four hundred Mexicans in the church, but a second time they were driven back from their forlorn hope.

On the morning of the second, firing was heard in the rear. Crabbe led a party in the direction indicated by the sound. He came upon a body of Mexican soldiers retreating toward the plaza before a small body of Americans. Hemmed in between two fires, they were cut to pieces. A moment later Captain McKinney was shaking hands with Crabbe. He had fought his way to Cavorca to join his chief. He brought word from Colonel Wood that he might be expected in a few days. The little band of invaders, hampered though they were by lack of provisions and ammunition and by their wounded, were in a flush of hope.

Gabilondo heard their cheers as the little bunch of filibusters under McKinney joined their comrades. His men had already suffered heavily and he knew that the Americans could not be taken without much further loss at best. So he sent a flag of truce, offering to allow the Americans to withdraw unhampered if they would leave the country. Crabbe declined the terms.

Gradually the numbers opposed to the filibusters told against them. As day after day passed, the little company of Americans became smaller. They were short of water, of provisions, and of ammunition, but still they kept the flag flying. Every day they looked eagerly for the expected reinforcements, but the leaden hours dragged away without the longed-for relief.

Meanwhile, the Mexicans, cutting through the walls of the intervening houses, drove the Americans back, fighting for every inch, to the last house in the row. Artillery and fresh reinforcements had been brought up by Gabilondo, who was in constant communication with Pesqueira. The pounding cannons were battering down the adobe walls. The food of the defenders had been entirely exhausted for nearly two days, and they had left only one keg of powder. This was the condition on the morning of the eighth day of the defense.

Crabbe sent out a flag of truce, offering to accept the terms proposed by Gabilondo a week before. But conditions had changed, and the Mexican commander now declined.

Crabbe gathered together his unwounded men— fifteen in all—and with his last keg of powder made a rush across the plaza to the church, bent on blowing up the church and its occupants. A heavy fire raked them from every side. Before they were halfway across the plaza three men had been killed and several wounded. Crabbe himself was shot in the elbow. Less than half of them, under a galling hail of bullets zipping against the stone walls and sidewalks, reached the church.

But they had to fall back at once to save themselves from being cut off. Carrying their precious keg of powder they returned to their adobe fortress. Seven wounded and three sound men staggered back from the abortive attempt.

But night fell with their spirits still unbroken. Sentries were set as usual. At midnight one of them aroused Crabbe.

"Sir, the roof is on fire," he said.

It was true. A Papago Indian had sent a flaming arrow against the thatched roof. Presently bits of burning thatch were dropping on the heads of those within.

There was a hurried consultation. Many of the men wanted to make a sortie and die fighting. But Crabbe remembered the promises of Pesqueira and clung to the hope that their lives would be spared. One Hines was dispatched to Gabilondo with a white kerchief of truce. Gabilondo sent back Cortelyou, a brother-in-law of Crabbe, to promise that they would be treated as prisoners of war and given a fair trial at El Altar. The men were to leave the building one by one without their arms.

Among those who did not want to surrender were Lewis and "Big Bill" Allen. The latter, badly wounded in two places, broke his rifle across the door in a rage.

"Surrender and be d——d," he cried. "We're going to our death."

Perhaps "Big Bill" remembered what had been done to the McLeod party, which had surrendered to General Armijo, governor of Santa Fe, on promise of friendly treatment not many years before; how a small remnant of them had been at last set free after brutal outrage, disease, and murder had thinned their ranks. Perhaps he recalled the Mier expedition from Texas, five hundred Anglo-Saxons who crossed the border in pursuit of marauders and were trapped into surrender. It had been Santa Anna himself who had ordered each tenth member of the party to be shot, and it had been Santa Anna who confined those left in loathsome dungeons till many died from disease, starvation, and cruelty.

In any case Allen's prophecy was well founded.

Fifty-eight gaunt survivors marched out of the burning building just before the roof fell. Among them was a boy of fifteen, "Charlie" Evans. They were bound and marched to the barracks.

This was at eleven o'clock in the evening. Two hours later a sergeant entered and announced that the whole party was to be executed at daybreak. The sentence was read in Spanish, but Cortelyou translated it to his friends. Col. R. N. Wood wrote down the names of the party and sent the list to the officer in charge of the Mexican troops, requesting him to forward it to their friends in the States. Crabbe and others also wrote letters to their wives and other relatives. These were never delivered.

Pesqueira had issued orders to Lieutenant Gabilondo to shoot down at once without trial any members of the Crabbe party captured by him. For long Gabilondo suffered under the obloquy of having massacred the prisoners. He refused to obey this dreadful order and instead resigned his commission in the army. Later Governor Pesqueira had him court-martialled for insubordination. Years later Gabilondo was a custom-house officer at Sasabi.

This tardy justice is due the memory of a gallant officer and gentleman.

The officer had Crabbe brought before him and promised him his life if he would tell where the looted treasure was buried. The Californian looked the butcher up and down, then turned scornfully on his heel.

"Take me back to my comrades," he said to the sergeant.

An hour earlier the boy Evans had been awakened from a sound sleep and led away. Gabilondo took the boy behind him on his horse and rode away to El Altar.

The haggard, bloodstained Americans were led out in squads of five and ten to the plaza, where they died by the fusillade after they had been robbed of their valuables. Not one of them begged for mercy.

After witnessing the execution of his men Crabbe was tied to a post and shot down. His head was cut from his body and exhibited in a jar of vinegar. Later it was forwarded to Pesqueira. Minister Forsyth reported the massacre to the United States government as "legal murder," and the government was satisfied. By the laws of nations it had to be.

The party of Col. Robert Wood had in the meantime ascended the Gila River to the Pima village, and from there had crossed to Tucson and Toboc to enlist recruits. Col. Charles D. Poston, a distinguished citizen of Arizona during its early territorial days, was at Tubac when the Wood party arrived there looking for reinforcements. He was at that time manager of the Sonora Exploring and Mining Company, which was opening mines that depended upon Mexico for its labour and its supplies. He had at the company store large quantities of arms, ammunitions, saddles, and wagons, as well as horses in abundance, together with a force of one hundred men. The adventurers tried to induce Poston to join them. He declined to do so, on the ground that it was an unlawful expedition against a friendly country, one calculated to disturb existing peaceful relations. Moreover, since he was laying the foundations of his own fortune, it would be absurd to go into such a hare-brained scheme with the resources he had at command.

Poston not only remonstrated with the leaders of the Wood party but rode to Calabasas to get Major Enoch Stein, who was in command of United States troops there, to urge him to arrest the intending invaders lest they bring about international complica-

tions and incidentally ruin the business of the Sonora
Exploring and Mining Company. The major declined
to interfere. He added that personally the filibusters
had his best wishes.

When Poston returned to Tubac he told Wood that
while he was against the expedition he would permit
his men to shoe horses and otherwise assist the party.

An old soldier, Colonel Douglass, then living at
Sopori, told the Wood party that they ought not to
cross into Sonora without enough men to whip both
of the political factions there, since it was certain that
Pesqueira would betray them.

The Americans were young, hardy, and courageous.
Moreover, they knew that Crabbe and his party were
expecting them and might be hard pressed. They took
their fortunes in their hands and crossed the line into
Sonora. There were twenty-seven of them, including
Wood and Tozier.

They travelled fast—this little forlorn hope of
riders. They reached the Altar district, were almost
within sight of Cavorca when they heard the fusillade
that ended the lives of their comrades.

Already they were hard pressed. Mexicans were
ambushing them from fields and arroyos. Gathering
troops began to hem them in.

The Mexicans were already in arms all about them.
There was nothing for it but a retreat. Several water
holes they reached were already ambuscaded, and it
was only with great difficulty that the party, harassed
by pursuers, made good their escape. At one of these
water holes in the desert they were so closely pur-

sued that they cut the stomach from one of their mules, washed it, and filled it with water. Then, marching by a short cut all night and day, they reached a water hole near the border.

More than once they had to fight their way through companies of Mexicans. They reached Arivoca in a terribly destitute condition—all of them worn out and many of them wounded.

So ended the last filibustering expedition from this country to Mexico.

Pesqueira took a terrible revenge on all those who had aided or were suspected of having encouraged Crabbe. Martin Ainsa was assassinated and his goods confiscated. Others were either shot down or driven out of the country.

Of the body under the command of Col. Robert Wood only two survive[1]. One of these is Major Tozier, the other is John G. Capron of San Diego, California. Major Wood died years ago. He served with distinction in the Confederate Army through the Civil War, and when the call to arms came for the Spanish War, the gallant old veteran slipped away from his family to St. Louis to offer his services to his old commander, Fitzhugh Lee. Of such heroic stuff were the old filibusters—impulsive, lawless, faithful, but filled with the fiery, chivalrous devotion of the South. They are a vanished race, faultful and unscrupulous, no doubt, but they had the fighting edge if ever men had.

[1]This was in 1904, at which time I visited Sonora and gathered the facts for this article. Both Tozier and Capron must long ago have passed away. W.M.R.

TOM HORN

An Enigma of the West. He Was Branded for
Murder and in His Later Years Was Known
as One of the West's Worst Bad Men. Yet There
Was Much Good in Him

TOM HORN was hanged in Wyoming, November 20,
1903, for the murder of Willie Nickell, a fourteen-
year-old boy shot down from ambush by an assassin
who evidently mistook him for his father.

The psychology of a bad man is difficult to understand, in the case of Horn peculiarly so. It is hard to
believe that one so liberally endowed with good qualities as this scout, one with a record so distinguished,
personality so outstanding, would have hired out to
do murder at so much a head. I do not know whether
Tom Horn did or did not kill Willie Nickell. The verdict of the court was that he did. As far as I know he
had a fair trial, and the sentence was in accord with
the evidence given. None the less, he was a frontiersman of great energy and courage, a loyal friend, a
faithful servant, given to generous impulses, and very
intelligent.

More than any other one man Tom Horn was responsible for the capture of Geronimo. After Al Sieber
was shot up by the Apache Kid, it was Horn who led

the scouts when they trailed the old raider for
months over many hundred weary miles and it was
Horn who went with Lieutenant Gatewood to his
camp and persuaded him to meet General Miles for a
peace talk. He was recommended by General Wilcox
for a government medal, both because of his courage
in rescuing Sergeant Murray under fire and for his
coolness and skill in saving troops in danger of becoming demoralized.

During the Spanish-American War, as master of
transportation with the pay and rank of colonel,
Horn was indefatigable in getting ammunition and
supplies to the front. He had 520 mules to be used as
pack animals. The transports could not get close
enough to the landing to disembark them. Meanwhile,
Roosevelt's regiment and others were marching in-
land depending upon this mule train. Horn got permission of Shafter to fling his charges overboard. All
but two of them swam to the beach. Through the hot
tropical hours of darkness the pack master and his
men toiled without rest, pushing their way through
the jungle trails to the front. They were at the scene
of action before the band began to play.

While Horn lay in prison before his execution I was
in the office of the United States marshal for Arizona
at Phoenix. A young man spoke up and said he would
give half of all he had in the world to save the condemned man. He had been in Bucky O'Neill's troop
of Rough Riders. Like so many others he became ill
with fever. A friend and he were lying out on a pile
of brush, both of them very sick men, when a big

brown-faced Westerner stopped to ask them where they were from.

"Arizona," one of them said.

That was enough for Tom Horn. He took them into his own tent, waited on them, fed them, nursed them. Ten days later he sent them back to their troop entirely recovered.

All over Arizona and Wyoming you could, in the old days, hear stories like this about Tom Horn. He was an open-hearted man. On one occasion a family of Russian immigrants got off the train at Greeley, Colorado. The children were ragged and barefoot. They looked half starved. Tom fed them and he clothed them. He returned them to their parents with their skins full and with new shoes on their feet.

Horn stood well over six feet in height. He was deep chested and lean loined, splendidly muscled, arrow-straight. A strong, hard man, one might have guessed, with truth. He was an excellent cowpuncher. On July 4, 1888, he won the prize at Globe, Arizona, for steer roping and tying. Later in the same year he won the mythical world's championship for the same event at Phoenix, Arizona, making a record of $49\frac{1}{2}$ seconds, a time never before beaten. (The conditions of contest have been so changed that it is not fair to compare modern records with this.)

There, then, is the record. Tom Horn, crack cowboy, first-class trailer, indomitable soldier, genial friend, kind-hearted neighbour, picturesque personality! Tom Horn, hired killer of "nesters"! Unbelievable but true, on the evidence presented. There is a queer kink (or was, for most of them are dead) in many of these game, hard-riding, friendly Westerners, the frontiersmen who each risked his life frequently and learned to hold it at small value. When in opposite camps they put the same valuation on the life of another. It is possible that Tom Horn regarded rustlers as pests and considered himself an executioner of justice. Possible, but hard to believe.

Tom was born at Memphis, Missouri, in 1861. His people were farmers, hard working and religious. The rest of the family, both brothers and sisters, were obedient and well behaved, but this one son was a vagabond and an Esau. He preferred to hunt coons and turkeys rather than go to church. He would play "hookey" any time to follow a rabbit. At the age of fourteen, after a very severe thrashing from his father, he ran away from home and headed toward the setting sun. Helping some freighters, he landed at Santa Fe toward the close of 1874. Employed by the Overland Mail Route, he drove teams, herded mules, and made himself generally useful. Presently he found himself in Arizona, at Beaver Head Station, near the Verde River.

The lad was big for his age and wholly self-reliant. He earned the wages of a man by doing a man's work. Later he was employed by the government to look after the mounts sent to Fort Whipple from California.

About this time Al Sieber, one of the most noted of army scouts, dropped into the fort and asked the boy to go with him to the San Carlos Agency to act as Mexican interpreter. Young Horn had picked up Spanish with much facility. He proceeded to do the same at the reservation with the Apache language. Sieber was much interested in him and taught the youngster a great deal about Indian habits and scouting. Tom learned also from Micky Free, a daredevil of a fellow, half Irish and half Mexican, whose parents had been killed by the Apaches. Free had only one eye, the other having been lost in a fight with a wounded deer. His hair was long and fire-red. Irish though he looked, Micky could not speak a word of English.

Sieber knew that if Horn was to become a good scout he must know Indians more than superficially. He arranged with Chief Pedro, who also had taken a liking to the sunny-tempered lad, for Tom to live with the old chief.

Pedro chose a young man as a friend for Tom, and henceforth the Indian brave was called Chi-kis-in, the native word for brother.

"You are an Apache now," old Pedro said. "My lodge is your lodge and my friends are yours. Hunt, fish, and trap with Chi-kis-in. There are many fine girls in my tribe, and some are ready now to throw a stick at you." (An Apache girl throws a stick at a brave if she likes him and he may then court her.)

Though Tom lived with the friendly Apaches he was on government pay. He learned to make rawhide ropes, to braid bridles, to fashion moccasins. The money of the Indian Department gave out, and the scouts were discharged. Al Sieber headed for Tucson, and with him rode a large bunch of packers and scouts, including "Buckskin" Frank Leslie, later one of the worst bad men of the border, "Wallapai" Clarke, famous as the man who put a period to the career of the Apache Kid, and of course Tom Horn.

At Tucson Ed Schieffelin was outfitting a party to go mining in what later became Cochise County. Some of the scouts joined him. Schieffelin had already prospected the Dragoons, the Whetstone, and the Mule Mountains, and he was sure that millions were waiting to be uncovered. He was right. Within a short time he discovered the mines that were to make Tombstone famous. Horn and Sieber located a claim and sold out for a few thousand dollars.

They had had enough of mining, and General Wilcox wanted them to join up again as scouts. Nana and Geronimo were off the reservation with their hostile braves. Sieber, Merijilda Grijola, and the boy Horn were detailed to get into contact with the Apaches and talk peace. Geronimo knew well and trusted Grijola and Sieber. A meeting was arranged.

Horn was to see this famous Apache chief many times when acting as a go-between, a messenger sent from the army chiefs to negotiate terms of surrender. He describes his first impression of the old man: an intelligent wily face, piercing eyes, and much given to bombastic talk which could not be trusted. But he looked every inch a fighter. The muscles flowed smoothly under his skin, and he was graceful as a panther. He stood six feet high and was splendidly proportioned.

In a book which Horn wrote while in prison before his execution he tells in great detail his experiences as a scout, but he barely mentions his life as cowboy, deputy sheriff, Pinkerton sleuth, and cattle detective. No reference is made to his Cuban record.

Sieber and Geronimo talked, or rather the Apache talked and the scout listened. The brave recited eloquently all the wrongs of himself and his tribe and told upon what conditions he would leave the warpath and return to the reservation. Sieber turned and walked away. Tom saw him later lying on his blankets and looking up into the sky. "Go away, boy," he said. "I'm thinking up all the mean things I can say to that old wolf to-night when we meet again."

After dark they returned to the council fire, three white men and three hundred blanket warriors fresh from the slaughter of scores of settlers. Sieber gave them plain talk. They could give up their evil ways and return to the reservation, or they could remain in their war paint and be hunted down by the troops. The whites, Sieber said, were like the leaves on the trees. There were hundreds of them to every Apache. If the Indians refused to yield they would be slowly exterminated. He told Geronimo that the chief was a man of war and not peace, that there was no hope of turning him to better ways, but if there were any in the camp who wanted to settle down he would take them back to the reservation with him.

All night the Indians talked among themselves. More than threescore Indians, including Mana and old Loco, returned to the San Carlos agency with

Sieber. The others followed Geronimo and turned their backs on peace.

For years Geronimo tricked both Mexico and the United States. Now he was in one country, now in another. He negotiated with Generals Wilcox, Crook, and Miles, always to his own advantage. When he decided to be a good Indian he and his braves would come across the line driving hundreds of stolen Mexican stock, promising reformation from that day. When he wanted to raid again he stirred up trouble at the reservation and took the Chiricahuas on the warpath.

During all these years Horn played an important part, first under Sieber and later as chief of scouts. Captain Maus, in the *Personal Recollections of General Miles*, says: "I cannot commend too highly Mr. Horn, my chief of scouts. His gallant services deserve a reward which he has never received."[1]

Occasionally the appropriations for the Indian Department gave out. At such times Horn mined, worked on cattle ranches, or served as a deputy sheriff. He acted as guide for Bucky O'Neill, when the latter as sheriff of Yavapai County took the trail

[1]Within the past few months, at Newcastle, Wyoming, I was shown various original Tom Horn documents, including the strong letters of recommendation written him by General Miles and other officers under whom he served. These are owned by my friend F. W. Hilton and came into the possession of his father, a well-known newspaper editor, in a very curious way. Mr. Hilton was attending by chance a sale of trunks and suitcases left unclaimed at an express office. He bid fifty cents for an old suitcase and it was knocked down to him. The name on it appeared to be Thorn, but an examination showed that it had belonged to Tom Horn, who had been hanged at Cheyenne a few days before the sale. A great many papers of interest to him were in the suitcase. He had never reclaimed it because his arrest and trial had prevented him from doing so.

after a bunch of train robbers and clung so close to them that several running fights were engaged in between the outlaws and the posse. In one of these two of the bandits were killed. Horn was an expert trailer and a persistent one. He stuck to the long chase, and at last Bucky came upon the rest of the gang in Wah Weep Cañon as they were sitting before their camp fire. A large sum of money taken from the express car was recovered, and the robbers brought back to Prescott.

Later, while serving with the Pinkerton Detective Agency under McParland, Horn was detailed to work with "Doc" Shores on another train robbery case. The Denver & Rio Grande Railway had been robbed near Texas Creek.

C. W. Shores was for many years sheriff of Gunnison County and afterward at the head of the D. & R. G. secret service. He is one of the few old-time fighting Western sheriffs still alive. I saw him yesterday, on a Denver street car, erect as ever in spite of his eighty-odd years. He is hawk nosed and his eyes blaze. I do not know how else to describe the keen glitter with which they rest on one.

A dozen posses were scouring the country. Tom Horn himself was arrested twice and taken in to Salida for identification. Presently the amateurs dropped out of the chase. Shores and Horn followed the trail across the Sangre de Cristo range, back by way of Mosca Pass, down the Huerfano Cañon, and east to Trinidad. From there the robbers went to New Mexico, got into a shooting scrape at Clayton, and crossed the line again, this time into the Panhandle of Texas. From Texas the trail led to the Indian Territory and down the Washita River. Here, near Paul's Valley, the trailers captured the two men, who were named Burt Curtis and "Peg Leg" Watson. The two men were tried in the United States District court and given life sentences in a federal prison.

It was the misfortune of Horn that he was of the old West and could not adapt himself to the new order. He gave years of his life to bringing law to the frontier, but when he had brought it he could not fit into the tamed communities he had helped establish. He knew Arizona when it was wild and woolly. A hundred times he risked his life to make conditions safer for the settler, but when law and civilization came to the territory he turned his back upon it. So it was with Wyoming. He saw the barbed-wire fence and the little red schoolhouse come. He saw the open range vanish. And he did not like the new conditions.

Tom had the vices as well as the virtues of his kind. He rode hard, fought hard, and toward the latter part of his life drank hard. Sober, he was a quiet, soft-spoken man, though when among friends not averse to telling of his experiences. Drunk, he boasted and told wild stories of his exploits. By his own account he had killed cattle thieves and made nothing of it. His reputation as a bad man grew, and perhaps it fed his vanity that this was so.

On one occasion Horn came to Denver and went on a spree. He had plenty of money with him and showed it foolishly. As he got drunker he became more boastful. There was more where that came from, he said. Tom had fallen in with two men who coveted the roll. One of them was a reporter, the other a prize-fight promoter. The men looked at each other, understood, and plied Horn with liquor till he was helpless. Then they frisked him. They secured five hundred dollars. Next day the newspapers told the story. One line in the account disturbed the crooks. It was that Horn knew who had robbed him. The reporter left town that day and did not return until after Horn had been hanged. He explained later that he did not know the drunken cattleman whose money he had lifted was Tom Horn. The mention of that name sent him on his travels.

About the beginning of the century there was much talk in a certain section of Wyoming that Tom Horn had been employed by cattlemen to wipe out rustling. The thieves had grown very bold, it is said. The nesters themselves tell another story. They say that they were in the way of big cattlemen who wanted the range. Men mysteriously disappeared.

There were complications. One Kels P. Nickell brought in sheep, and this is a deadly wrong in a cattle country. Already there was bad blood between his family and a neighbouring one named Miller. This had reached the proportions of a feud.

Willie Nickell was found dead on the prairie, not far from his home, in July, 1901. Two days prior to this time Horn had spent the night at the Millers'. For some time no arrest was made.

The Nickell sheep made trouble. In August Kels

Nickell was shot, but his wounds were not serious. Later his sheep were clubbed.

Joe La Fors, a deputy United States marshal, came into the case. He became friendly with Horn, who was now drinking heavily. At Cheyenne he planted witnesses in the marshal's office and led Horn on to talk. Tom thought there was a job as stock detective in the offing, and to show that he would go through for his employers told La Fors that he had killed Willie Nickell and several rustlers. To the last Horn denied that he had made such a confession, claiming that he was framed by the officers.

Horn had staunch friends. One was a cattleman, John C. Coble. Another was a schoolteacher who lived with the Miller family and told a strange story of a confession on the part of another than Horn. Scores of men and women in Arizona and Wyoming and Colorado believed him innocent. The preponderance of evidence was, however, against him.

John C. Coble penned a last tribute to the scout.

The story is done. Close the pages that tell of fighting our country's foes, of secret service, of Cuban campaigning, of zeal, of faithfulness, of fearlessness. Unwritten always must remain the record of Tom Horn's bravery, loyalty, generosity, and the countless kindly acts which marked his pathway through life. I am proud to say that he was my friend, always faithful and just. When can I hope to see such another! And no man ever walked more bravely to his death. I am convinced, and I reassert it to be true, that Tom Horn was guiltless of the crime for which he died.

Perhaps. Let us hope so, for Tom Horn had much good in him.

HELLDORADO

Stories of Arizona's Wild Old Days, When You Couldn't Keep a Bad Man Down

BE IT understood, to begin with, that Tombstone never was a bad town. I have this on the authority of several old-timers who lived there in its high-stepping prime. William M. Breakenridge says so, and he ought to know, for more than any other man in the camp, he carried law into the mesquite. The quiet-spoken ex-frontiersmen who may be met at the Pioneers' Society headquarters at Tucson will tell you the same.

Not a bad town. There were no holdups or burglaries. People who minded their own business were left strictly alone by the gunmen. Women were as safe as though they were in God's pocket. The gamblers were good citizens, and the wives of some of them were leaders in the church; for professional gambling was as legitimate a business as selling groceries.

A nice, quiet, clean town! When you got up in the early morning you could hear the song of the crissal thrasher, sweet and well modulated. You walked on the top of the world, beneath an intensely blue sky, in an enchanted atmosphere, and breathed air exhilarating as champagne.

Beyond the roll of hills and valleys, with their cholla and prickly pear and greasewood, rose the Dragoon Mountains, and the Mules, the Burros, the Whetstones, and Huachucas. You met miners with dinner buckets going to their work. You saw clerks sweeping out stores. Smoke rose from the chimneys of adobe houses, where mothers were calling children to get ready for school. A drooping horse stood by the hitch rack in front of the Alhambra. A hound lay in the pleasant sunshine and hunted casually for fleas.

The sound of a shot shattered the stillness, followed by an explosive fusillade. Out of the Alhambra burst a man, smoking .45 in hand. He ran limping to the horse, flung himself into the saddle, and galloped down the street in a cloud of dust. Inside the hall a man lay face down on a table among a litter of chips and cards. Another looked with pained surprise at the blood dripping from his pistol fingers. There had been an Arizona difference of opinion.

Tombstone knew such differences on the part of leading citizens. They were known tactfully as "difficulties," and the result of them as "killings." The word "murder" was harsh and offensive. There was one such difference when Curly Bill, leader of a very active band of rustlers operating in and near the Dragoons, shot Marshal White while being arrested.

There was another when Luke Short fought a duel with Charlie Storms in front of the Oriental gambling house, and left his man dead in the street. Storms was one of the best-known gamblers in the entire

West, and Short already had several notches on his gun. They were dealers at rival houses. Very likely they did not like the colour of each other's hair.

There were preliminary hearings, for this was, as has been noted, a quiet, law-abiding town. In the case of Curly Bill, testimony was given by Virgil Earp that the affair had been an accident; and in the second instance Bat Masterson came to the defense to show Storms the aggressor. Cases dismissed.

Frank Leslie, known as Buckskin Frank, had a reputation as a killer. So had Billy Claibourne, a cowboy who had worked for John Slaughter. Frank was tending bar for M. H. Joice, at the Oriental, when Billy came in, the worse for liquor, and made himself offensive. He was ejected. Naturally, he went away, armed himself with a sawed-off shotgun, and lay in wait with intent to relieve the world of Buckskin Frank Leslie. A friend brought word to Frank that the boy was stationed behind a fruit stand, ready for action.

Leslie put down on the bar the cigar he was smoking, examined his .45, and stepped quietly out of the side door, from which he soft-footed to the front along the adobe wall, caught sight of his man, and mildly called out, "Billy!" Claibourne turned, and a moment later pitched forward on his face, a bullet through his heart. The bartender returned to his duties, picking up the cigar still smoking on the bar. Mr. Leslie made comment, as he polished the black walnut top, "He died nice."

Some of the old-timers still alive regard Buckskin

Frank as the worst killer in Arizona's history, as the most dangerous man with a six-shooter who ever came to the territory. He was so quick on the draw that most bad men were content to treat him always with the respect that made a quarrel impossible. He and Joice held a ranch in the Chiricahuas, one of the best-known in the country. Here he fought several duels, and at Galeyville he engaged in others, always to the misfortune of his opponents. It is said that he killed more than a dozen men in single combat. Leslie was a scout, and during the last campaign against Geronimo worked under Major, afterward General, Lawton.

Buckskin Frank was a quiet cold man, yet both vindictive and passionate. He made the mistake of shooting at the ranch a woman of whom he was jealous. For this he was sent to the penitentiary for a long term.

Take the case of ex-United States Marshal Duffield, an old-timer who had kinged it at Tucson long before Schieffelin located the Tombstone, before the Toughnut, the Visina, the Grand Central, and the Contention were sending forth their millions. He was a picturesque old ruffian, Duffield, the only man in Arizona or western Texas who dared to wear a plug hat in the early days.

Mr. Duffield did much as he pleased. He was chain lightning on the draw. Every day he drove a ten-penny nail into an adobe wall at twenty paces to make sure his hand had not lost its cunning. There were thirteen notches on his guns. In height he stood six foot three. He was broad shouldered, powerful, muscular.

Ordinarily he was a pleasant, quiet-spoken citizen, but when in drink he was disputatious and overbearing. Most men took one look at him—at his splendid physique, his black hair, his keen black eyes—and withdrew tactfully from any possible discussion.

But in some affray Duffield was wounded in such a way that his nerves were shattered. He recovered, in a measure, but he was a changed Duffield. This was in the '70's, when time was marked by events rather than by the calendar; as, for example: "The night afore Duffield drawed on Judge Titus," or, "The night Pete Kitchin run the tinhorn outa town."

Duffield moved to Tombstone and tried to ruffle it bravely as of yore, but a young man named Holmes put a swift period to his career.

It will be admitted by the old-timers that Tombstone, "not a bad town," was yet not a staid New England village. Every building on one side of Allen Street was a saloon or gambling house, and these never closed, day or night.

Wild games were played, with twenty-dollar gold pieces for chips and the roof for a limit. Keno, chuck-a-luck, roulette, faro, and poker offered diverse entertainment, while bands flung music into the night. If one tired of the Crystal Palace, or Hafford's, there was the Bird Cage Theatre, where Eddie Foy could be seen, and where blonde Junos, working for the house, were willing to smile kindly on one while drinking champagne.

At Schieffelin Hall, if one inclined to the classical, Frederick Warde and Charles B. Hanford offered Damon and Pythias to a none too exacting public. The Can-Can Restaurant catered to palates both fastidious and the reverse. The Daling Saloon in its advertisements stressed by implication the gentle nature of its clients: "Call Frequently, Drink Moderately, Pay on Delivery, Take Your Departure Quietly." Could anything be fairer?

But if Tombstone was a nice, quiet town in which to bring up children, the same indorsement cannot be given all of Cochise County. The rich Tombstone mines had brought hard characters from all over the country. Dodge City and Abilene had struck twelve and turned good. But they contributed "Doc" Holliday, Bat Masterson, Luke Short, the five Earp brothers, and many others to the new Helldorado.

Mark Smith, for very many years the representative for Arizona at Washington in the House and the Senate, says that in 1881 he could have counted forty killers in Tombstone, most of whom had done their killing elsewhere. It must be remembered that the population of the place was only sixty-five hundred and that there were a hundred law-abiding citizens to every gunman. Tombstone was not bad; but Cochise County—gentlemen, hush!

Some of the toughest characters that came to Cochise were the buffalo skinners. They had taken the buffalo without price and they undertook to do the same with cattle. Wild young Texans poured into Cochise, cowboys filled with hatred of the Mexicans on account of the history of the Lone Star State. Missouri and New Mexico were doing belated house-cleaning. It was in 1881 that Jesse James and Billy the Kid were killed.

These sections offered their quota of toughs. In wagons, by stages, on horseback, they turned their faces toward Cochise County. Lincoln County, New Mexico, at its worst, and Texas in the palmy days of Sam Bass, had nothing on this southeast corner of Arizona in the years '80, '81, and '82. Lest I seem to exaggerate, let me quote from an Arizona paper dated a year or two later: "In the dark days of Cochise County, when our carnival of hell was in full blast . . ."

Incidentally, the issue of the Tombstone paper referred to mentions only one killing, one stabbing affray, one stage robbery, and one Apache outrage since the date of previous issue.

There were few cattlemen in the county as yet, and their ranges were poorly stocked. When four or five boys drove up a likely bunch of longhorns, few questions were asked. It was quite possible the boys had been "swinging a wide rope." Very likely they had raided into Mexico and run the herd from the range of some señor who lived in feudal style on a Sonora hacienda. What was the difference?

Galeyville, near the Chiricahua Mountains, on the rim of the San Simon Valley, was the hangout of the rustlers. They spent their time drinking and gambling here when not operating. When their money was gone they went off on another raid into Mexico for more cattle. These they might bring up by way of Guadalupe and Skeleton cañons into the San Simon Valley.

The rustlers had squatted in the gulches, near water, and had built corrals there. Here they divided the stolen stock, rebranded the cattle, and resold to convenient buyers at attractive prices. The Mexicans at first were not prepared to resist these invasions. Later they made ready. Pitched battles were fought, with many casualties.

These rustlers had their code. They were wild and lawless. Sometimes they robbed stages. Occasionally, while drinking, they killed one another. But in the main they were easy-going likable young fellows, few of them more than twenty-three or -four years old.

Mexican smugglers were doing a rather lively business on the border. Between El Paso and Nogales there was no port of entry, and it was easy to smuggle adobe dollars into Arizona and American goods back. There was, be it mentioned, an export duty on silver and an import duty on merchandise. The cowboys often fell on these bands of smugglers and robbed them, sometimes after a fierce fight. Life was cheap on the border, and killing a Mexican did not count.

They tell a story on old Jerry Barton, constable at Charleston in 1880. Jerry was a killer, and he and Jim Barnett, J. P., ran that corner of Cochise. Someone asked Jerry how many men he had killed. Jerry was given to stuttering. He reflected a moment, and then asked, "D-do y-you c-count M-mexicans?"

Old Man Clanton and his sons, Finn, Ike, and Billy, had a ranch on the San Pedro a few miles above Charleston. The McLowrys[1] had one in the Sulphur Springs Valley, four miles south of Soldiers' Hole. It is claimed that the Clantons looked after the interests of the rustlers on the San Pedro, and the McLowrys took charge of the stock brought up through Agua Prieta (where Douglas now stands) into the Sulphur Springs Valley.

Old Man Clanton ran one bunch of cattle too many across the line. Mexican vaqueros dry-gulched him and his cowboys not far from Tombstone, and left none of them to tell the tale.

The real leaders of the rustlers were John Ringo and Curly Bill (the latter legally known as William Brocius or William Graham, according to the fancy of the moment). Ringo was well educated and liked to read good books. He was at times morose and moody. When in liquor he could be quarrelsome. He was fearless, a good shot, and his word could be depended upon absolutely. He stood six foot two.

Those who knew him were impressed by the pathos of his blue eyes; when in repose there was always sadness in them. It was written in his face that he would come to a tragic end, and he did; but just how he came to it, no man knows. He had been drinking heavily, and continued to do so as he rode out into the burning desert.

There are two stories. One is that he took off his

---

[1] The relatives of these young men spell the name McLaury. In Tombstone days it was as given in the text. W. M. R.

boots, hung them on the saddle, and went to sleep; that when he awoke, the horse was gone; that he tore off his shirt to protect his feet from the hot sand and the stinging cacti; and that at last, tortured by thirst, he put a bullet through his forehead. The other is that Buckskin Frank stalked Ringo, found him in drunken sleep, and shot him while he was defenseless.

Curly Bill was of another type. He, too, stood more than six foot in his boots and was built like a fighting man. His hair was black and curly, his face freckled. He was an amiable man in the main, and he could relish a joke, even on himself.

On one occasion he and his crowd attended church at Charleston. It was observed that the congregation began to filter away. The minister hesitated as to what was best to do. Curly Bill explained that he and his friends had not come to make a disturbance. Whereupon the pastor changed his text. He preached on the theme that they that take the sword shall perish with the sword. Curly passed the hat and saw that it was filled. Never before or since has that church seen such a collection.

Next day, Barnett, justice of the peace, met Curly, trained a rifle on him, and fined him twenty-five dollars for disturbing the peace at church. The outlaw paid, but he announced that in future he would have to stay away from church. It was too expensive for him.

As time went on it was inevitable that some of the rustlers would turn their attention to the rich shipments of bullion going out from the Tombstone mines. Among those suspected of stage robbery were Frank Stilwell, Peter Spence, Jim Crane, Harry Head, and Billy Lennord. The names of Zwing Hunt and Billy Grounds have also been mentioned; they were known rustlers and suspected road agents.

It became observable that the stage was never held up except when there was a gold shipment aboard. The wise drew deductions. Somebody in Tombstone was giving notice when bullion was to be shipped.

The Earps were officers of the law, at least some of the time. Virgil was city marshal at Tombstone. Wyatt held a place as deputy United States marshal. Morgan rode for Wells-Fargo as a shotgun messenger. James, the oldest of the five brothers, ran a saloon. Warren was still a boy, though later he followed the family tradition. (He was dealing faro years later in an Arizona mining camp and was killed by one of the rough characters in camp. Some say the man that shot him was Burt Alvord, an Indian trailer, deputy sheriff, and train robber, whom I knew in Arizona thirty years ago. Burt was one of the few outlaws who left Arizona alive. When last heard of, he was headed for the Argentine.)

They were large men, the Earps; strong, bold, and fearless. With them as allies might be counted Doc Holliday, Luke Short, and others, including Bat Masterson during his short stay in Tombstone. They were a dangerous combination, for the group stood as a unit.

Wyatt Earp was a leader. He had the qualities that

go with that position, the driving force necessary in such a frontier community to set a man apart as one of mark. Bat Masterson has set it down that he once asked Wyatt why he was so friendly to "Doc" Holliday, a morose, quarrelsome man far too quick on the trigger, and that Earp answered that his friendship was born of loyalty because Holliday had saved his life at Dodge.

In any case the friendship was an expensive one for the Earps. Rightly or wrongly, Holliday was accused of complicity in the attempted hold-up of the Sandy Bob stage near Drew's Station on the way to Benson.

Bud Philpot, the driver, had changed seats with Bob Paul, the shotgun messenger. The stage was moving easily through a rocky defile when a crisp "Hands up!" brought it to a halt. Masked bandits ranged up beside the Concord. A shot or two was fired to intimidate the passengers and the guard. Then, with no provocation whatever, one of the outlaws, a slight man, fired two shots with fatal results. One killed Bud Philpot, the second pierced the heart of a passenger riding on top of the stage. The horses became frightened and ran away, so that the robbers got nothing.

The rumour spread that the masked killer was Doc Holliday. He was an embittered man, a consumptive, always too quick to shoot. As soon as the news of the hold-up reached Tombstone, Johnny Behan, the sheriff, set out to trail the bandits, with Frank Leslie, Bob Paul, and Billy Breakenridge.

Marshal Virgil Earp, with his two brothers, Wyatt and Morgan, also organized a posse. The trailers started from Drew's ranch in the San Pedro Valley, followed eighty miles down the San Pedro, crossed the Catalinas within fifteen miles of Tucson, around the foot of the range to Tres Alamos, thence to Helm's ranch.

The trail winked out, but Behan's posse, augmented by the Earps, headed toward New Mexico.

There are two stories of the inside facts leading to the tragedy that followed. Both of these were sworn to later in court, one by Ike Clanton, the other by Wyatt Earp. It became known that Crane, Head, and Lennord had been with Holliday at the robbing of the stage, but that the killing had been unforeseen by them.

According to Ike Clanton, Wyatt Earp admitted to him that Holliday had done the killing, and proposed to Clanton to assassinate the other three robbers to prevent them from telling what they knew in case they were caught.

Earp's story was that he wanted Ike Clanton to trap the three men so that he, Earp, might get the credit of arresting them in order to help his campaign for the office of sheriff. The latter story seems more likely than the former.

Both of the stories agreed that Clanton was to get the $6,000 reward that had been offered for the bandits, dead or alive. Ike was of opinion, however (so he later swore), that if he fulfilled his part of the contract he would die suddenly, as dead men tell no tales.

The rustlers believed Ike Clanton's story. They felt that Earp and his gang were prepared to betray them to protect Doc Holliday. Bad blood began to brew between the cowboys and the Tombstone group. Each side made its threats.

In the meantime, before the difficulty reached the proportions of a feud, the stage that ran between Tombstone and Bisbee was held up and robbed by two masked outlaws. Billy Breakenridge and Dave Nagle were sent by Sheriff Behan to track the outlaws. This was the same Nagle who, many years afterward, shot David Terry, formerly of the California Supreme Court, while acting as a guard for Justice Field.

The bandits had covered their tracks by driving cattle across them, but they had been indiscreet. One of them had joked the passengers during the robbery by asking if they had any sugar. It was known that Frank Stilwell commonly used this word to mean money.

Breakenridge then did a fine piece of detective work. He found Frank Stilwell and Pete Spence at Bisbee. They seemed to be close pals. Breakenridge had checked up tracks found in the sand at the scene of the robbery. He talked with a shoemaker at Bisbee and learned that Stilwell, after the hold-up, had had the heels taken from his boots and others substituted. The shoemaker produced the heels he had removed, and these fitted the tracks at the place of the hold-up.

The suspected men were arrested. The Earps interfered. As deputy United States marshal, Wyatt claimed the right to take the bandits back to Tombstone. He did so. This increased the bad feeling between his gang and the cowboys.

The Bob Hatch saloon was the hang-out of the Earp faction in Tombstone. Word came to them that the Clantons and the McLowrys were in town.

Perhaps they had come "to get roostered," that is, to have a wild time in the metropolis of Cochise. Perhaps business had brought them. No doubt they intended their enemies to know that they were not afraid to come into their bailiwick.

They were hard-riding young outlaws, these cowboys, good shots, and in every way first-class fighting men. But in strategy they were no match for those opposed to them.

The plan of the town faction at first may have been to protect themselves, but after Ike Clanton had a difficulty with Doc Holliday in a poker game, they evidently made up their minds to force the issue. Perhaps they felt that war was inevitable and that it would be wise to see that they got the breaks. Virgil Earp, the marshal, and his brother Morgan followed Ike, knocked him down, disarmed him, and haled him before Justice Wallace, where he was fined for carrying concealed weapons.

Before the justice arrived, Ike had words with

the Earps, several of whom surrounded him. According to his testimony later, they taunted him.

"Fight is my racket, and I only want four feet of ground," he told them.

Wyatt handed him a gun, the muzzle toward him. At the same time Virgil and Morgan watched him closely, the latter with his hand inside the breast of his coat. Ike knew a trap was laid for him, or so he swore later, and declined the immediate issue. This was Clanton's story.

Next morning Wyatt Earp met Tom McLowry. They exchanged smoking epithets. Earp knocked the other down with the barrel of his pistol. McLowry said he was unarmed. Men led him away, stunned and bleeding.

It must have occurred to the cowboys that they were not equipped for a clash. They made preparations to leave town. Their horses were at the O. K. corral. They finished what business they had, and saddled leisurely. But they let the precious minutes slip away, possibly in a spirit of bravado, more likely because they did not anticipate a massed attack.

Sheriff Behan was in a barber shop when word reached him that trouble was impending. He got through as quickly as possible and found Marshal Earp on Hafford's corner. Behan urged the marshal not to push the issue. Virgil's answer was:

"They are looking for a fight and they can get it."

He carried a shotgun, the muzzle touching the door sill. Morgan Earp and Doc Holliday were standing at Fourth and Allen streets.

The sheriff hurried down to disarm the cowboys. If he could do so and take them prisoner, there would be no immediate trouble.

The rustlers came out of the O. K. corral, two of them leading their horses. Behan asked Frank McLowry for his gun. McLowry said they were leaving town and objected to giving up his weapon unless the Earps also did so. Ike Clanton and Tom McLowry were not armed, and said so.

Behan knew now that he had only minutes left in which to arrange an armistice, for the Earp party could be seen coming down the sidewalk on the south side of Fremont Street below the post office. The sheriff moved quickly toward them and met them near Bauer's butcher shop. He tried to stop them, explaining that two of the cowboys were unarmed and that they were leaving town. There were four in the Earp party—Wyatt, Virgil, Morgan, and Doc Holliday. They pushed past the sheriff toward the corral.

Marshal Earp spoke brusquely: "You're under arrest. Throw up your hands."

Three of the cowboys did so. The fourth, Tom McLowry, threw open his coat and said that he was unarmed.

The two parties were now standing within six feet of each other.

Almost instantly two shots rang out, so close together that they could not have been fired by the same person. Doc Holliday, carrying a nickel-plated pistol, got into action first and Morgan Earp next according to the preponderance of testimony. A fusillade followed. The cowboys made a game fight.

Tom McLowry clung to the horn of his saddle to keep from falling while he tried to unstrap a rifle fastened there. Frank McLowry and Billy Clanton answered the fire turned on them. Both were already wounded to death and knew it, but they fought as long as they had strength to lift their six-shooters.

Billy Clanton, a boy of nineteen, was the last to go down. He stood against the adobe wall of an assayer's office and kept shooting as his body slowly slid along the wall to the ground.

The battle lasted scarcely thirty seconds. When the guns no longer sounded, both McLowrys were dead or dying. Billy Clanton was so badly riddled that he lived scarcely an hour. Morgan Earp was slightly wounded. Ike Clanton had escaped by way of Fly's photograph gallery. They say that Wyatt Earp let him go, seeing that he was unarmed. "Wyatt was the best of the Earps," an old-timer told me recently. He was certainly the most remarkable, and there is no evidence whatever to show that he ever took pleasure in killing.

This was on October 26, 1881. After a long hearing, the justice dismissed the case, alleging self-defense. The editor of the *Nugget* had the courage to come out in an editorial with the statement that the sentiment of the community was that justice had not been done.

Some weeks later Virgil Earp was shot at and wounded by someone unknown. He recovered.

The rustlers were not yet through. Nearly five months after the affair ot the O. K. corral, Morgan Earp was killed in Bob Hatch's saloon, the Bank Exchange. He was playing billiards at the time. A bullet fired from outside had crashed through a window to reach him. It was discovered that someone had piled up two boxes and stood on them in order to see his victim.

Spence and Stilwell, the stage robbers arrested by Breakenridge, were known to be in town. They were out on bond, awaiting trial. Spence proved an alibi as to the killing. Stilwell vanished from sight at once, riding hard for Tucson. Two Indian woodchoppers with him also disappeared.

The Earps started with Morgan's body for California. With them went Doc Holliday, Sherm McMasters, and a man named Johnson. They entrained at Benson and reached Tucson. Two men saw the train draw into the station. One was Ike Clanton, and the other was Frank Stilwell.

Said Ike warily, "They're aboard; we better light out."

He did. Stilwell lingered. It is believed he was hoping for a shot at some of his enemies. No chance offered. He turned and walked down the track, unaware that he had been seen.

When Stilwell's body was found later, an examination showed that four rifle bullets and two loads of buckshot had been pumped into it.

The Earp party returned to Tombstone.

Sheriff Behan, standing in front of the Cosmopolitan Hotel, saw them come up. All of them were heavily armed.

"Wyatt, I want to see you," Behan said.

"You'll see me once too often," Wyatt answered darkly.

None the less, Wyatt knew that it was time to be gone. There were fifty cowboys in the hills ready to avenge the death of their friends. To walk the streets of Tombstone was dangerous. To take a *pasear* into the surrounding country would be an invitation for an ambushing.

Grimly the Earps and their friends rode out of town. Toughnut Street knew them no more. Never again did they dominate the Alhambra, the Crystal Palace, or the Oriental. Arizona's loss was Colorado's gain, if you want to put it that way.

But first they had business afoot. At Pete Spence's camp they stopped to collect the "breed" suspected of aiding Stilwell in the killing of Morgan. They found him chopping wood. His body was found a few hours later.

They rode warily, keeping continual guard against surprise. Once they met a bunch of cowboys, Curly Bill at their head. There was a long-distance fight, known by the rather grandiloquent name of the Battle of Vurleigh. The Earps claimed they killed Curly Bill. Perhaps they did. At any rate, he vanished from the scene of his operations.

The Earp gang rode far. They had a good friend in Denver, and for that city they headed first. Bat Masterson met them and extended the glad hand.

It chanced that Bat had never liked Doc Holliday, but for his friends' sake he made him welcome, too. Masterson was a respected citizen in Denver, and he found that he needed all his influence to protect the Tombstone emigrants.

Arizona demanded the return of the trekkers. Bat went to Governor Pitkin and pleaded their case. To send them back to Cochise would be judicial murder, he claimed, since they were wanted there by their enemies and would be sacrificed without a fair hearing. Moreover, Doc Holliday was wanted by Colorado for highway robbery. Why give him up to Arizona? This last was true, in a manner of speaking. Bat arranged a dummy holdup and filed charges against Doc Holliday as the guilty footpad.

There was some colour to Bat's argument. It was plain to the Colorado governor that if the Earps went back to Arizona there would be bitter and bloody warfare. And Governor Pitkin had reason to believe that Arizona had its tongue in its cheek when it asked for their extradition. He had been privately told that a refusal to give them up would simplify the territorial situation. Therefore he declined to honour the demand for extradition.

The Earps went their several ways, most of them to California. Doc Holliday died a few years later of consumption in Colorado.

The departure of the Earps from Tombstone was the beginning of the end. Cochise County began to get unroostered. The cattlemen had a change of heart. They sheltered and protected the cowboys while the latter were running Mexican stock across the border. But when, this grown dangerous, the rustlers turned to local product, the cowmen sided with the law.

Behan and Breakenridge and subsequent sheriffs drove the young outlaws hard. John Slaughter, a small, beady-eyed frontiersman, devoid of fear, served notice: "Rustler, get out if you want to live."

Billy Grounds, short and red-faced, tied up with Zwing Hunt, a tall, slim dandy, in nefarious cattle transactions. Breakenridge captured them after a desperate fight in which one of his posse and one outlaw were killed and the other outlaw was badly wounded. The rest of the posse was more or less wounded.

Billy Grounds had come to the ordinary sudden end of his kind. Zwing Hunt, still suffering from a bullet hole in one lung, took to the hills with his brother. An old-timer once gave this advice in Indian days: "When you see 'Pache signs, be keerful; when you don't see 'em, be more keerful." The Hunts were not "more keerful," and the Apaches jumped them. Zwing fought them till he died. His brother escaped on a hobbled mule.

So the outlaws found the net of the law closing on them. The Anglo-Saxon has a passion for law and order. It may come slowly, but come it does—the wiping out of the bad man.

Six young men of southeastern Arizona discovered this too late. They were the John Heath gang of rustlers who had been operating in the Sulphur Springs

Valley. They had pulled off a holdup or two in Clifton and had made the place too hot for them by killing a man.

The six of them dropped into Bisbee one day by twos and singly. At some agreed-upon signal they gathered at the mining company store and robbed it. Several of the men went inside while others stayed on the street. The alarm went out and the outlaws began to shoot. They killed a passing citizen and also a woman named Roberts, who was standing in front of her restaurant. A deputy sheriff from out of town, by the name of Smith, moved toward the outlaws, perhaps under the impression that they were playful cowboys. One of the gunmen asked him who the hell he was, and when he said he was a peace officer the outlaw drilled him through the heart. Two others were wounded.

Five of the outlaws rode out of town. The sixth, John Heath, joined the posse being organized to follow the bandits. He was recognized, arrested, and taken to Tombstone. The other five escaped for the time. They scattered in all directions, after they had reached the Chiricahuas.

Two of them, Jim Howard and "Big Red" Sample, slipped back to Clifton and hid on the Blue River. One of them had made the mistake of telling a dance-hall girl where they were going. Olney and Hovey, deputy sheriffs, surprised them and brought the two robbers back to Clifton. A third bandit, Dan Dowd, was run down in Chihuahua, Mexico, and a fourth called Bill Delaney, in Sonora. Dan Kelly was the only one of the six still at large. He was arrested on a train near Lordsburg, New Mexico, by Anton Mazzanovich, the author of *Trailing Geronimo*, assisted by two other citizens.

John Heath secured a separate trial and was found guilty of second-degree murder. The other five, tried in a group, were sentenced to be hanged. The miners objected to Heath's sentence and lynched him in front of the Last Chance mine. The other five were later hanged by process of law. Sheriff Ward made the event a holiday and issued invitations to the hanging. The prisoners died game. One of them advised the sheriff not to make a mistake and hang the priest instead of one of the outlaws. The five men were buried in Tombstone's famous Boot Hill Cemetery.

The night riders of Cochise rode no more. Law had been carried into the mesquite.

LAW WEST OF THE PECOS

The Famous Lincoln County (New Mexico)
War from Which Billy the Kid and Sheriff
Pat Garrett Emerge as Two Supermen of the
Six-shooters

TO BEGIN with cattle was an adventure rather than a business, an investment which travelled on the hoof unwatched and unguarded, subject to obliteration by disease, drought, exposure, and the cupidity of man. By the simple process of rebranding, one's drifting capital or the dividend therefrom might any day change ownership. A rustler put his brand on a neighbour's calf. It became his own. The Texas fever swept a stretch of country, and cattle died as by a plague. So my father's herd vanished within a week. Decidedly cows were an adventure.

The genesis of this attitude toward cattle was in the conditions produced by the Civil War. The men of Texas were in the Confederate army. For years cattle were neglected, were left unworked. They had no value. A plug of tobacco was a standard price for a good yearling. When the soldiers returned to their homes they found the country filled with cattle running wild, great numbers of them unbranded. To prove ownership was usually difficult, often impossible. Therefore these longhorns came into possession of the men who most energetically claimed them. The foundation of more than one fortune was built on a rope, a fire, and a running iron.

Out of these conditions rose John Chisum. He was a cattleman of vision, and when Western markets began to develop he turned his eyes from Abilene and Dodge and Ogalala to Denver and Vegas and Tucson. With characteristic boldness he pulled up stakes in Texas and moved lock, stock, and barrel to New Mexico. He drove his great herds up the Pecos and built several ranches. One of these was near the present site of Roswell, another on the river at Bosque Grande, a day's ride north of this.

Chisum waxed exceeding fat. His herds multiplied, grew so great that he himself did not know the extent of his holdings. He kept open house like a feudal lord, and like a baron of old he had many enemies.

All along the river, especially toward the north of his holdings, were nesters, small cattlemen ranching on their own. They did not like the way the Jingle Bob spread everywhere and took the best grass and water. They objected to the arbitrary methods of the Chisum retainers, saw no reason why he should be king of the New Mexican range. On his side Chisum returned their dislike. He found fault with the rate of increase of their herds and charged that they rustled his cows and calves wholesale.

They were hard-bitten Texans, most of them, veterans of the Civil War. Under the leadership of Major L. G. Murphy they drew together.

Murphy was an old army officer who had gone into business at Lincoln, the county seat of a district almost as large as Illinois. He owned cattle. He built a store, ran wagon trains, filled army contracts. With his partners Dolan and Riley he controlled the trade of a wide territory. Ranchmen on the Hondo, the Ruidoso, and the Bonito came to him for advice, credit, and support. He was the big man of the mountains, just as Chisum was of the Pecos Valley.

They did not like each other, these two barons of Cattleland. Busybodies went to and fro carrying tales of what was said and done, fanning distrust to active hostility.

One Alexander A. McSween, a lawyer, had settled at Lincoln in the middle '70's. He was of a legal turn of mind, wholly unfitted for leadership among the scores of desperate men soon to be engaged in deadly warfare. But circumstances and his own ambition forced him into at least nominal command of one faction. He could dictate general policies and did, but it was not in the man to exact obedience from such hardy ruffians as Dick Brewer, "Doc" Skurlock, and Billy the Kid. Having sown the wind, he had to reap the whirlwind.

This was an Apache country, and the settlers who had ventured into it were fighting men. Each of them carried law in his own holster. Cattle thieves nested in the hills. Outlaws ruffled it on the streets. Wall-eyed gamblers plied their trade in the saloons with reckless cowpunchers and freighters as customers.

In the years of its wild youth it was day all night at Lincoln.

For instance, there was the "Harrold War," just concluded before McSween and his bride reached New Mexico. The Harrolds came from Texas, down Lampasas River way, and there they were known as Horrell. (It was characteristic of the frontier that the names of men, even when not changed because the owner was on the dodge, suffered variant spelling in different localities.) There were five brothers of the family, Sam, Mart, Tom, Ben, and Merritt. They were cattlemen, well respected at Lampasas before they "went bad," though they were recognized as men quick on the draw when stirred to anger.

Lampasas in the early '70's was a wide-open town, frolicsome and exuberant. The Harrolds frequented Jerry Scott's saloon on the west side of the square. Occasionally they and their friends shot up the town by way of amusement. Some of the townsmen, not amused, appealed to Governor Davis for help. He sent five of his state police to put a stop to it. Davis was a Republican, a carpet bagger, and negroes were enrolled in his constabulary. Therefore they were unpopular.

Captain Williams, in charge of the squad, left a coloured constable with the horses and trailed with the others into Jerry Scott's place.

The troopers were white men, named respectively Daniels, Cherry, and Melville. According to the account of James B. Gillett, a Texas ranger famed for his skill and courage, there were a good many men in the saloon at the time, including Tom, Mart, and Merritt Harrold. Some were playing pool. One was picking a banjo. It was a gay and carefree crowd before Captain Williams stepped into the room, but with his coming the atmosphere changed. The eyes of the cowboys and cattlemen fastened on him. They seemed to be waiting for a cue.

Williams had been drinking. He walked to the bar and ordered whisky for his men. His eyes circled the room, came to rest on a revolver on the person of Bill Bowen, a brother-in-law of one of the Harrolds. Intrepid but unwise, he announced harshly that Bowen was under arrest.

"You can't make that go," Matt Harrold drawled.

The officer's six-shooter leaped out and barked. Matt Harrold staggered back, badly wounded. That shot was a signal for action. Revolvers blazed lanes of fire through increasing veils of smoke. A dozen weapons were out at once.

When the guns ceased speaking Captain Williams and Daniels were dead on the floor of the saloon, Cherry lay breathing his last outside, and Melville was dragging himself, fatally wounded, to the porch of the Huling House. The coloured policeman was spurring wildly for safety.

Within twenty-four hours Lampasas was full of soldiers. The wounded Harrold and Jerry Scott were arrested. The rest of the Harrolds, their relatives the Bowens, John Dixon, Ben Turner, and others of their allies went on the dodge. But not for long. The Harrolds gathered their forces and made a night attack on the jail to which the prisoners had been transferred. After a fierce fight, during which a prominent lawyer named A. S. Fisher was seriously wounded, the two prisoners were released and carried away.

The Harrolds and their friends departed for New Mexico, driving their herds before them. They went openly and defiantly, sending word to the sheriff at Lampasas the day and hour they would pass through the Gap. Nobody molested them.

They settled in Lincoln County, on the Hondo River. Their experience at Lampasas had not tamed them. On a moonlight night they rode across to Lincoln, accompanied by Ben Turner and the Bowens and shot up the town. There was always plenty of law in Lincoln County, though it cannot be said that justice was blindfold. Usually, open-eyed, it took one side or the other.

So now the law, in the persons of Constable Martinez and former Sheriff Gillam, assisted by two or three citizens intent on calling the Harrold bluff, disputed the right of way. Later, when Lincoln counted the casualties, it found Gillam, Martinez, and another resident dead. Along with these was Ben Harrold.

Not many days later the Harrolds returned, appeared at a Mexican *baile*, started trouble, and left four men and one woman dead, not to count the wounded. There was a good deal of bushwhacking after this between the Mexicans and the Harrolds. Several Mexicans vanished inconspicuously. Ben

Turner was shot down. All told, more than fifty died in the Harrold War.

Again the Harrolds found the country too hot for them. They returned to the scene of their former activities. Briefly, to round out their turbulent careers, I mention that in Lampasas County they engaged in a feud with the Higgins family and adherents, also cattlemen. Merritt was killed in the Jerry Scott saloon. In the counter attack Mart was badly wounded. Furious battles followed, in which men were shot down on both sides. The surviving Harrolds were killed by their enemies while in jail.

This digression serves to illustrate the character of the community McSween was attempting to rule with a statute book and a Bible, aided (so his enemies say) by chicanery. Definite opinions concerning the guilt of the leaders in the Lincoln County War should be offered cautiously. They were products of the conditions, in part at least. Most of the survivors are partisan or speak on hearsay evidence. Official New Mexico, as represented by its papers and those in authority there, favoured the Murphy-Dolan-Riley faction. Newspapers were divided in the counties contiguous to the warring district.

At first McSween acted as attorney for Murphy, but the two men were incompatible. They broke with each other and became bitter enemies. On behalf of Chisum the lawyer prosecuted men charged with rustling Jingle Bob stock. This was resented by Murphy. The Fritz estate was another bone of contention. Fritz had been a partner of Murphy. At his death he left considerable property and ten thousand dollars of insurance. Murphy claimed Fritz owed him money. As lawyer for the heirs McSween refused to recognize the claim. The Murphy faction charged that McSween was robbing the estate and putting the profits in his own pocket. There was a missing will, and other melodrama galore.

At Las Vegas, on his way to St. Louis, the lawyer was arrested and flung into jail, charged with embezzlement. This was in January, 1878. Later he was released, having been admitted to bail to appear before the district court of Lincoln County.

McSween wrote a long letter to the Cimarron News & Press denying that he had been running away. He made counter charges against Murphy. It is an incongruous note of this cattle war, the most savage and ruthless in the history of the country, that most of the leaders of the different factions sent lengthy epistles to different papers protesting against the lawless practices of the other side. Murphy, Dolan, Riley, McSween, and several of their subordinates and alleged nonpartisans wrote such letters. You may read them to-day in the old files of the Santa Fe *New Mexican*, the Mesilla Valley *Independent*, the Mesilla *News*, the Grant County *Herald*, and the Trinidad *Enterprise*. Outraged virtue sticks out of every paragraph of them.

Prior to this time McSween, in partnership with J. H. Tunstall, had built a store to compete with the Murphy one. He had also started a bank, of which John Chisum was president.

Tunstall came of a wealthy English family. The natives referred to him derisively as the Belted Earl. He had come to New Mexico because he loved the outdoors and was fond of big-game hunting. His ranch was on the Feliz, a short day's ride from Lincoln. The freedom of the life delighted the genial red-faced Englishman. He did not care whether people laughed at what they thought his idiosyncrasies, for he knew they liked him. Poor Tunstall was the most tragic figure in the war. He went his happy, care-free way, serenely sure that all the little differences of opinion would be smoothly ironed out, don't you know. To the moment of his cowardly murder he had no fear of these savage "warriors" who could kill without compunction. As a matter of fact, he refused to believe such fairy tales. They did not seem to him reasonable. He was a competitor of Murphy, to be sure. He did not like the man, but he had no hatred of him. It was all in the day's work. Let the best fellow jolly well win. Tunstall was as out of place in such a business as was McSween and much less a responsible factor in the situation.

He would not see that a bitter war was at hand in which scores of lives might be lost and no quarter would be given. Rake Texas and the Southwest with a fine-tooth comb and one could not have gathered together a more lawless and desperate body of partisans. The court of last resort was the six-gun, and most of these range riders were adept pleaders. Gunmen snuffed out lives as carelessly as one might a candle. If it was dangerous to be a partisan, it was none the less so to attempt to remain neutral, for such killers as the notorious Jesse Evans, Tom Hill, Dave Rudabaugh, Ike Stockton, Tom O'Folliard, Dick Brewer, and Charlie Bowdre were likely to count any man an enemy who was not a friend.

Into this welter of desperate humanity sauntered one day its future king. His name was William H. Bonney, alias William Antrim, known later as Billy the Kid. By grace of natural fitness he was to become chief, because he was the worst bad man that ever strapped on a six-shooter in the West.

It makes for dramatic effect that this most ruthless of desperadoes was a slight pale lad, small-boned, with the high piping voice and the genial friendly smile of an amiable cherub. We are moved to wonder that among so many superlative ruffians one so young could have achieved preëminence, for he was cut down at the age of twenty-one, when most boys are just leaving school, having snuffed out twenty-one lives, by his own admission.

The Murphy faction started the war by an atrocious cold-blooded murder. To collect the debt he claimed against the Fritz estate Major Murphy levied on McSween's property. It was claimed the lawyer had turned his assets over to Tunstall to avoid an attachment. From Lincoln rode a very large posse under command of W. S. Morton, a deputy sheriff, toward the Rio Feliz.

Word reached the Tunstall ranch that more than twenty men were on their way toward it. Dick Brewer, foreman for the Englishman, urged strongly that those present decamp at once. Tunstall refused to go. Why run away like curs when there was no need of it? Precious hours were wasted in argument. At last Brewer got his chief mounted and headed toward Lincoln. With the small party rode a deputy United States marshal named Robert A. Widermann. Billy the Kid was one of the Tunstall party.

The Morton posse stopped at the ranch and collected the stock. James J. Dolan, a partner of Murphy, stayed here with some of the men. The others rode with Billy Morton after Tunstall. The dust of their horses' hoofs could be seen for miles in the untempered atmosphere.

Brewer saw that cloud of dust at a distance. He knew what it meant. Another long wrangle with Tunstall began. The Englishman refused obstinately to run. He was, he said, no criminal trying to escape justice. In vain Brewer and the others pleaded with him. The dust cloud grew nearer. Brewer announced bluntly that he was not going to throw his life away because his boss was a fool. Even then, according to Widermann, who wrote an account of the affair later published in the newspapers, Tunstall's friends did not leave him without having to fight a rearguard action to escape.

Tunstall jogged along, not quickening his pace in the least, though by now he must have suspected that he was in great danger. He even stopped as the posse drew near and greeted some of its members by name. So far as is known he had never had an unpleasant word with any of them.

A shot rang out, and he fell from his horse. Tom Hill jumped down, put a rifle to the fallen man's head, and blew out his brains. The murderers made a mocking jest of their ghastly deed and went on their drunken way. Frank Baker, a bad man and an outlaw, was one of those present. It is said, on dubious evidence, that Billy Matthews was another. The preponderance of evidence is that Matthews stayed at the ranch with Dolan.

The Tunstall murder was like a match to a powder magazine. Hired warriors were brought up from Texas to join one side or the other. Feeling ran so high that it was dangerous to be a neutral. Scores of armed men rode in compact groups the streets of Lincoln, one group watching another with wary, smouldering eyes. There was bound to be a clash soon. It did not come in town. Perhaps neither side was yet worked up enough to precipitate a general battle.

Law, I have written, did not follow a split line of justice in Lincoln. Sheriff Brady was a friend of Murphy and of Murphy's friends. McSween went to John P. Wilson, justice of the peace, and had Brewer appointed a constable. Whereupon Brewer, a hard-eyed fighting man intent on avenging the death of Tunstall, summoned a posse and set out to arrest the murderers. In that posse rode "Doc" Skurlock, Charlie Bowdre, Fred Waite, Frank McNab, Billy the Kid, Jack Middleton, a Smith, a Brown, and one McClosky, who had no place in such a company.

The posse rode far. At the lower crossing of the Rio Penasco they jumped five horsemen, who fled at once. There was a running battle. Three of the fugitives separated from the others and took to the hills. Brewer's party followed the two. The horses of the hunted men were killed. The two dismounted riders reached a dugout and stood off the posse until their ammunition was spent. They hoisted a handkerchief, after many hours of battle, and bargained for their lives. Brewer agreed to protect them. They surrendered.

It is probable that both Morton and Baker, looking around on the cold savage faces of their enemies, knew that they were marked for death. With some of these men they had exchanged pleasant badinage around the camp fire of more than one cow camp. Baker at least had ridden crooked lawless trails with young Antrim and probably with Charlie Bowdre and "Doc" Skurlock. Not two months before this time several of these warriors had been in the Murphy pay. (Billy the Kid, for one, had jumped recently to the McSween side.) But these things counted for nothing now. They had killed Tunstall and must themselves die to pay a debt of vengeance.

The two prisoners were taken to the Chisum ranch and spent the night there under guard. Both of them took occasion to send letters and mementoes to friends in the East. These they left with the lady of the ranch, a niece of John Chisum. It had become quite clear to them that they would never look upon another sunset.

Yet it is pleasant to relate that one man in that posse of killers valued his honour more than his life. He was a gnarled old-timer named McClosky. While the horses were being saddled Morton prophesied to Baker that they would never reach Lincoln alive. He made the prediction before half a dozen of his captors. There was a moment's silence. Someone laughed, a jeering cruel laugh. Then McClosky declared himself, and in one sentence lifted himself from the killer to the hero class.

"They can't kill you two boys while I'm alive," he said quietly.

The words were his death warrant. By lonely, unfrequented trails the party headed toward Lincoln. Three horses with empty saddles were turned into the corral at the Bowdre ranch late that night. In some silent gulch Morton, Baker, and McClosky were shot down. Later, details were whispered here and there. Members of the posse had been drinking heavily. One and another of them argued with McClosky to change his mind. He was obstinate, though he knew the consequences of his stand. Who killed him nobody knows for sure, though Burns in his *Saga of Billy the Kid* names Frank McNab as the murderer. It is generally believed that Morton and Baker were slain by the eighteen-year-old boy who afterward became notorious under the name of Billy the Kid.

Events were moving fast. Tunstall was killed about the middle of February, 1878. Since then all Lincoln County had become an armed camp, though hundreds of decent citizens went their quiet ways resolved to join neither side. It was known by all that neither faction was ready to sign a treaty of peace. Each was awaiting a favourable opportunity for action.

Monday morning, April 1st, Sheriff Brady and his deputy George Hindman, accompanied by the clerk of the court Billy Matthews and George Peppin, set out to open court. Judge Bristol had not arrived, and the opening of the term was to have been merely a formal one. As the men moved down the street toward the courthouse they passed the McSween-Tunstall store.

A crash of exploding cartridges shattered the sunny silence. Brady fell dead. Hindman staggered forward and lurched down into the dust. Matthews and Peppin scudded for an adobe cabin and reached it. The accounts differ as to where the assassins were hidden. One story is that they were lying on top of the McSween house, another that they lay behind an adobe wall running parallel with the road and extending from the McSween store.

Billy the Kid had come by many evil trails to this hour of ambush. He had, at the mature age of twelve, knifed a man to death in a saloon row. With another companion he had killed three Indians who were pursuing him for running off a bunch of their horses. In Tucson he had quarrelled with a gambler and beat him to the draw. Another gambler named José Martinez had fallen before his deadly fire. By this time he was known among the killing fraternity as "a bad man to monkey with." If possible they avoided difficulties with him. The killer treads a precarious path. He must continue to live up to his evil repute, in order to terrify others who would like to gain éclat by putting an end to him. Continuously he must walk to and fro, a living invitation as target for ambitious rivals as well as honest law officials.

But it is worthy of note that the notoriety of this young desperado was as yet not widespread. He was not the fighting leader of his faction. The first mention of him I find in any newspaper is in the *New Mexican* of April 13, 1878. In the account of the Brady killing it mentions the fact that one Antrim ran out to the road and gathered up the weapons of the dead sheriff, and that in so doing he was seriously wounded by Matthews. In later issues of this and other papers he is referred to as "the Kid." Not till later did he become universally known as "Billy the Kid."

Score one to the credit of Ike Stockton, gambler, bad man, and killer. From the door of his saloon he saw Hindman lying in the hot sun and heard him begging for water. At last he could stand the sound of that piteous appeal no longer.

"Damn 'f I don't take a whirl at it," he said.

Stockton knew his life would turn on the flip of a card. There were men in the McSween store, watching the road, who were no friends of his. He unstrapped "the hogleg" from his waist, so that no man could say afterward that he was armed. Then, with a pail of water, he walked steadily out to where the dying man lay. He stooped down and gave Hindman water. The deputy drank, then his body sank into itself and he died. Ike walked back to the saloon, moved strongly by a repressed desire to run. At any moment a bullet might crash its way between his shoulder blades. The Kid and his friends let him go.

Hindman died within a few hours.

The newspapers say that John Chisum and Alexander McSween rode into Lincoln from the Chisum ranch, where McSween had been visiting, while the dead bodies still lay on the road.

The implication, hardly warranted by the known facts, is that these men were not only indifferent to what had occurred but had actually instigated it. Their guilt was less direct. But one thing stands out like a sore thumb. The business of a killer is to kill. When Murphy on one side and McSween on the other hired outlaws and Texas warriors to support their respective causes they put themselves out of court as pleaders for right and justice. It may be said that the only way to fight force was by force. This is to beg the question. McSween could have disposed of his holdings, for some fraction of their value, and left the country rather than engage in open warfare which must cost many lives. Game men have done this in many parts of the West in preference to committing themselves to a course not approved by their consciences. During the Tonto Basin War, in Arizona, many settlers pulled up stakes and departed, choosing to do this at heavy cost rather than accept the alternative of joining either the Graham or the Tewksbury faction.

Though a partisan, Sheriff Brady had the reputation of being a good man. The Masons at Santa Fe passed resolutions of respect and sympathy after his death. These were signed by Max Frost, Thomas B. Catron, and David J. Miller. Frost was later the famous blind editor of the *New Mexican* and Catron a member of the United States Senate. In those troublous days a public official at Lincoln had to take sides. Naturally he leaned to his friends, the men who had put him in office, rather than to his enemies. But there is no reason to believe that Brady knew Billy Morton's posse would kill Tunstall. The murder of the sheriff was even more cold-blooded than that of Tunstall, because the killers were not inflamed by drink. They deliberately lay in wait to slay.

McSween, his brother-in-law W. P. Shields, and the deputy marshal, Widermann, were arrested for the dual murders and taken to Fort Stanton. They were presently released. Of the three only Widermann was accused of having taken direct part in the murder of Brady, and it is probable that he was not present. McNab is credited with having been the leader of the party. Billy the Kid, Tom O'Folliard, and Charlie Bowdre were almost certainly there, as was also Fred Waite, since he was wounded along with the Kid when the two ran out to the road to get Brady's weapons.

The McSween faction, for the moment in the ascendency, elected John N. Copeland sheriff, and during the brief period of his incumbency he took orders from the lawyer. Murphy appealed to the governor of the territory, Samuel B. Axtell, to oust Copeland on the grounds that he was a tool of Mc-Sween and refused to arrest the murderers of Brady and of Morton. The governor removed him on the technical charge of not having filed his bond within the required thirty days. In his place he appointed George W. Peppin, who had been a deputy under Brady, familiarly known as "Dad" Peppin.

It is a curious trait of human nature that even the most lawless like to move under the cloak of authority, no matter how shadowy it may be. I knew of a lynching party in Texas which broke into a prison and found its intended victims armed with chair legs. The prisoners could not be seized without great danger, since they were bold, hardy men. They could easily have been shot down, but the attackers could not bring themselves to do this. In their minds they drew a shadowy line between hanging and shooting. One could be considered the justice meted by a vigilance committee. The other somehow took on the colour of murder. So in the end the prisoners escaped.

Likewise, during all the lawless proceedings of the Lincoln County War, both parties were at great pains to move under some pale colour of authority. So it was when "the regulators," as they were called, on the morning of the fourteenth day of April, rode up to the Indian Agency at Blazer's Mill. Dick Brewer, named deputy constable by Justice of the Peace Wilson, was in command of the thirteen men who rode with him. It is worth while setting their names down, for that day they took an inglorious part in the most amazing battle ever known to have occurred in the West. They fought a cripple. Shot through and through, his death only a question of hours, a little man known as "Buckshot" Roberts stood off these fourteen hardy desperadoes and forced them to leave the field to him. That story is an epic of the West.

Andrew L. Roberts leaves few facts about his life to historians. His claim to fame has to rest on his one great hour. He had been a soldier in the United States army and probably a Texas Ranger. He was known as "Buckshot" Roberts because, like his more noted namesake General "Bobs," if you stood him on his head you could spill a pint of lead out of his crippled body. His arms were so badly shattered that he could not lift a rifle to his shoulder to take aim.

But there was the soul of a hero in that crippled little body. Many years ago, writing in the *Pacific Monthly*, I said that Roberts had announced himself a neutral in the Lincoln County War. So the old settlers told me. I see no reason to revise this opinion, though those who try to justify Billy the Kid and his friends now set him down as one of Murphy's hired killers. In any case, the story of his death has become an epic in a country which has forgotten a thousand game fights.

There was a story current at the time that Constable Brewer and his thirteen law officers had come to Blazer's Mill to get Judge Warren Bristol, who was expected there on his way to Lincoln. This has been denied. Whether or not it is true, the story at least reached the newspapers. It is not certain that this imposing body of gunfighters rode so far merely to bump off one unimportant cripple. This seems hardly likely.

Not long before this time Roberts had taken up a ranch on the Ruidosa. George and Frank Coe each had a place on this creek. Bowdre and Skurlock owned another jointly. They had bought it from Fritz and Murphy, and the Major complained bitterly that he had carried them for years and that now they were fighting against him. These men were neighbours of Roberts.

Yet the two Coes, as well as Bowdre and "Doc" Skurlock, were in the party that rode up to the agency and asked for dinner. The other regulators were Dick Brewer himself, Billy the Kid, Jake Scoggins, Steve Stephen, John Middleton, Tom O'Folliard, Jim French, Hendry Brown, Frank McNab, and Fred Waite. A coroner's jury, sitting on the body of "Buckshot" Roberts, found that he came to his death from gunshot wounds at the hands of eleven of these men. O'Folliard, French, and Brown were not named in the report.

Dr. Blazer ordered dinner for his uninvited guests. The meal was served and the men sat down to eat. I sat in the living room of Frank Coe's ranch on the Ruidosa seventeen years ago, and he told me the story of that fight. The opposition papers at the time charged that when Roberts rode up to the mill on his old mule Frank Coe was sent out to engage him in talk until the others could surround the old soldier. Coe says that he went out as a neighbour and warned

Roberts to light out or surrender, and that he took no part in the subsequent battle. If Coe's story is true—and I know of no facts to controvert it—there were only thirteen able-bodied men to fight the crippled soldier, *after he had been mortally wounded by a shot which traversed the bowels.*

Dr. Blazer and Major Godfrey, the Indian agent, were present throughout the fight. Mrs. Godfrey pleaded for the life of Roberts, a stranger to her, both before the attack and while the intrepid soldier was holding the doorway of Blazer's room. She might as well have begged mercy of a pack of wolves.

Roberts was sitting in a doorway of the house when the killers closed in on him. He rose, knowing he had come to the end of the passage. A rifle hung loosely in his hands. They called on him to surrender but waited for no answer. Charlie Bowdre's first shot fatally wounded the little man. Roberts fired in answer, and the bullet struck the buckle of Bowdre's belt. The other gunmen opened on their victim. He stood in the doorway of Dr. Blazer's room and kept his rifle going. Actually, according to the testimony of survivors, "Buckshot" Roberts outfought and out-gamed the whole outfit. One of his shots drilled Middleton through the lungs; another wounded George Coe, cutting the trigger finger from his hand. The attackers retreated out of range, leaving the wounded soldier victor.

The defender bolted the door and dragged himself through the house to the front door. He found weapons in the house, a six-shooter and an old Sharp's buffalo gun. These he appropriated for defence. He dragged mattresses to the door and built a protective barricade.

For hours he stood off the attackers. Brewer ordered Dr. Blazer and Major Godfrey to drive the intrepid soldier out of the house. They refused.

"I'll burn the place down if you don't," Brewer told them, exasperated.

"I wouldn't," Godfrey said drily. "The United States government might object."

Brewer swore he would have the man or know why. He crept down, under cover, to the mill and took up a position back of a pile of logs. He and Roberts exchanged shots. The wounded man behind the mattresses knew he had not many hours to live. He was in dreadful pain and burning up with fever. But he concentrated his whole attention on one thing—to get Brewer when the cowman raised his head. He took a long aim, his rifle resting on the window sill, and waited for the head to show. The distance was nearly two hundred yards.

Tunstall's foreman raised his head. A rifle cracked. Brewer dropped back dead, shot very neatly between the eyes.

The redoubtable posse had had enough. Their leader dead, four of them wounded, the heart for battle went out of them. What was the use of going on with this? Roberts would die in a little while, anyhow. They mounted their horses and rode away. Hard, rough fighters they were, but the dying man behind the mattresses was too good for them.

"Buckshot" Roberts died next day.

In passing it may be mentioned that only one of those who killed Roberts was ever indicted, only three of those who ambushed Sheriff Brady and Hindman, and none of those who slew Baker, Morton, and McClosky. But, after all, indictments were merely bits of paper which produced no results.

The McSween faction had been having things its own way. Six men had been shot down in reprisal for the murder of Tunstall. The Murphy adherents began to take a hand. But first the government troops rode into the drama and out of it again. Lieutenant Smith of the Ninth Cavalry, under orders from Colonel Dudley at Fort Stanton, had brought pressure on Copeland to arrest, with the aid of soldiers, seventeen of the Murphy adherents and eight of the McSween faction. In a day or two the twenty-five arrested men were back with their friends.

During all this time a good deal of sniping was going on. Cowpunchers were "dry-gulched." The horses of vaqueros came home with empty saddles. Men were missing from the ranches of Chisum, of Murphy, and of Riley. The wives of nesters waited for them in vain. There was guerrilla warfare over a wide stretch of country. Men rode with a wary eye the red hill shoulders dotted with jack pine and cedar. They crept furtively into gulches, not knowing when they might hear the crack of a hostile rifle.

The Murphy-Dolan-Riley faction had the law with them now. Sheriff Copeland was out and "Dad" Peppin was in. The new sheriff, sweeping the hills

with a score of Pecos cowboys, jumped Frank Mc-
Nab, Frank Coe, and one Saunders. Peppin wanted
these men. Particularly he wanted McNab, who had
been active in the three killings which had claimed as
victims Morton, Baker, McClosky, Brady, Hindman,
and Roberts. The three trapped men made for their
horses and "lit a-runnin'." Peppin pursued. This
was at the junction of the Bonito and the Ruidosa.

McNab's horse was shot, and a moment later he
was killed. Saunders fell, badly wounded. Coe was
captured uninjured. Wallace and Bob Ollinger brought
him in. The posse rode into Lincoln. There was a
long-distance battle, in the course of which one
Murphy follower was wounded. Coe was released by
Wallace Ollinger who had been set to guard him. Perhaps Ollinger did not care to be a party to a repetition
of the Morton-Baker-McClosky tragedy. They say
Wallace was a kindly man, very different from his
relative Bob, who comes again into this story later.

This opéra-bouffe battle was merely a preliminary
to the very real one which took place July 17th, 18th,
and 19th. By this time Lincoln County was achiev-
ing national notoriety. The fight had been carried
to Washington. Governor Axtell was under fire. An
investigation had been started which resulted later
in his removal from office and the appointment of
General Lew Wallace, of Civil War and *Ben Hur*
fame.

There was a hurried secret massing of troops, if
one wants to use that word in connection with the
cold-eyed brown-faced men who rode at the beck of

McSween, Chisum, and Dolan. There was a general feeling that the decisive clash was to take place within a few days. Billy the Kid, with half a dozen companions, rode up from Roswell. McSween brought in twenty-five or thirty Mexicans under Martin Chavez, though these did not arrive until after the battle had begun. Chavez, by the way, had been a Copeland deputy. Both sides were still trying to masquerade as law-abiding citizens. Sheriff Peppin was in nominal command of the Dolan-Riley forces.

Peppin's men used the Murphy buildings as barracks, the store, the hotel, and their stables. A rocky mountain side runs steeply down to the main street of the town. Behind the trees and boulders sharpshooters had been posted. The other faction was stationed in the McSween buildings. The latter was at first much outnumbered. When the Mexicans arrived some few of them slipped into the store, but most of them took up their quarters farther down the street.

The first day was spent in sniping. Also the second. There was only one casualty. A Peppin man, stationed well up the hillside, was killed by a Mexican sharpshooter. Neither party wanted to rush the barracks of the other, though there was talk of it on both sides.

Mrs. McSween and other women appealed to Colonel Dudley to stop the fighting. He marched in from the fort with some Gatling guns and two companies of troopers. The colonel's conduct was much criticized later, was indeed the subject of an official inquiry. He took the point of view apparently that

Peppin was an officer engaged in the lawful business of arresting criminals. Technically he was, but in fact both sides were engaged in factional warfare. Dudley summoned McSween to surrender, and the lawyer refused. Dudley then trained his Gatling guns on the headquarters of Chavez and told the Mexican that if his men fired a single shot the troops would get into action. He added that the deputy and his men had better leave town. Chavez took the hint.

With McSween were Billy the Kid, Charlie Bowdre, Tom O'Folliard, "Doc" Skurlock, Jim French, George Coe, Harvey Morris, a man named Brown, and several Mexicans. Mrs. McSween, an undaunted woman, was in and out of the house half a dozen times during the battle.

It became apparent that the McSween men were doomed. Colonel Dudley's men stood aside and watched the battle. The store was fired, and though the men inside tried to put out the flames they were unable to do so. They retreated to the farthest corner of the building. Billy the Kid was the fighting leader of the party. McSween was of no use in such an emergency.

The flames crept nearer. The trapped men must either make a run for it or burn up like rats. They threw open the door. McSween was the first to appear. His enemies were waiting for him. He went down before he had gone five yards. The other men tumbled out pell-mell, running for the adobe wall back of the house. Morris and two Mexicans were killed; another one badly wounded. The rest of the

McSween men got away in the darkness and reached the hills.

But they did not leave wholly unavenged. During that short rush their guns were busy, too. Bob Beckwith was killed, some say by Billy the Kid. But in such a mêlée there is no certainty as to what rifles and six-shooters carried death.

General Wallace had been appointed governor to stop the Lincoln County War. It died out, so far as actual fighting went, because the leaders were dead or bankrupt. McSween had been killed. Murphy had died a few days earlier. The hired killers departed, wages no longer being forthcoming. Wallace issued a proclamation of amnesty to all who had been engaged in the war, provided they were not under indictment for crime, conditioned on their laying down their arms. The governor arranged a meeting with Billy the Kid at Santa Fe and promised him that if he would surrender for trial a pardon would be given in the event of conviction.

But Billy was a born outlaw. He turned his back on this offer and resumed practice as a rustler and free-lance killer. Such men as Bowdre, Scurlock, O'Folliard, and Middleton stayed with him as members of his gang. Within ten days of his talk with the governor he killed an Indian agency clerk named Bernstein, for no reason except that the clerk had interrupted him while he was stealing horses. It was an unnecessary, cold-blooded murder.

Yet, strangely enough, this smiling, friendly boy who snuffed out human life as you or I might shoot a rat had friends during his lifetime and has apologists to-day. Some of the friendships were probably based on fear, but undoubtedly many people actually liked him. For one thing he was gay and genial and boyish. He could be the best of company. Nor was he of the mean cowardly type who would turn snarling on a friend, the sort who would start wilding up to prime himself for a killing.

Mrs. Lesnet, who was living at Roswell, New Mexico, a few years ago, knew the young outlaw well. She was living at Dowlan's Mill while Billy was being hunted. If one did not mind Indians and men on the dodge one could live a royal life in that wild country. In those arroyos, where the hills slid together, were deer and wild turkey in plenty. The rancher raised his own hogs, beef, chickens, and vegetables. Supplies were brought in from Vegas and Cruces by freight outfits drawn by oxen. A doctor travelled a district of a hundred miles in breadth. Nobody sent for him except on serious cases. The healthy outdoor life did not make for sickness.

So the young wife and mother was happy. Men passing to and fro always stopped there. Billy the Kid was often her guest. He had a little dog trained to stand still while Billy shot around its body. When he travelled the lad carried the little dog in front of him on the saddle.

Billy was courteous and pleasant. He paid for what he got. He made of the baby a great friend and used to say, "Mrs. Lesnet, let me hold him a while." Nevertheless, he always sat, when at table, with his back to a corner, so that his eyes could take in both door and windows, and while he ate a rifle lay across his knees. Eternal vigilance was the price of life for Billy those days.

There came a time when Billy Bonney visited her house under less happy circumstances. He was a prisoner, on his way back to Lincoln to be hanged. He had been tried for the killing of Bernstein and acquitted, then tried for the murder of Sheriff Brady and convicted. According to I. M. Bond, clerk of the district court at the time, Billy had treated the trial as a spectacle designed for his amusement. He took no more interest in it "than I would in a hand organ and a monkey," as the clerk put it. When Judge Bristol repeated the impressive formula, "And you are sentenced to be hanged by the neck until you are dead, dead, dead," the boy leaned forward and chanted defiantly, "And you can go to hell, hell, hell."

So Billy came to Dowlan's Mill, apologetic to his friend as usual for making her trouble. One of the guards was Bob Ollinger, a long-haired two-gun man who had functioned on the Murphy-Dolan-Riley side during the Lincoln County War. According to Emerson Hough, who undoubtedly derived his information from the famous sheriff Pat Garrett, the man Ollinger was both cowardly and murderous. He had a lust for killing prisoners and more than once had to be driven from his prey. Now, having Billy in his power, he taunted him continuously. He had jeered at him from the hour when he had gone to trial.

Not an hour passed, except when they were asleep, that Ollinger did not thrust savage irony at him.

"You'll come to Lincoln on the big day, won't you, Mrs. Lesnet?" the deputy asked, an eye on his prisoner to see how he took the remark. "Everybody'll be at the hangin', looks like."

"Everybody but me," Billy said, smiling over at his hostess.

"Shame on you, Mr. Ollinger, for talkin' so to the poor boy," the ranch woman said.

"Don't worry about me," Billy assured her placidly. "They can't hang me if I'm not there, can they?"

"You *will* be good if you get away, won't you, Billy?" pleaded Mrs. Lesnet.

But this is to anticipate. Billy the Kid, as I have written, after the termination of the Lincoln County War set up for an outlaw pure and simple. In addition to his former companions he had with him new associates, rustlers all, such men as Tom Pickett and Bill Wilson and Dave Rudabaugh. The antecedents of these men are not important. Rudabaugh will do as an example. He had robbed a train at Kinsley, Kansas, and had been captured by Bat Masterson, then sheriff of Ford County, Kansas, of which the county seat is Dodge. The bandit had later drifted West, not for his health, had killed the jailor at Las Vegas, and had been drawn to Billy's gang as inevitably as steel filings are to a magnet.

The gang operated in the Panhandle, on the Canadian, and on the Pecos. Hundreds of head of cattle changed hands. Pat Coughlin was always ready to buy without asking embarrassing questions, as Siringo has made clear in his latest book.

By this time the name of Billy the Kid had become a household word in the territory. He was the most expert killer the West has ever known, considering his age. Long before this he had quarrelled with John Chisum and had declared a vendetta against the cattle king. It is said that he dropped into a cow camp in the Panhandle one day where some young fellows were cooking supper. He accosted one, who was hobbling a horse.

"What's yore name, Texas man?"

"Bennett Howell."

"Who you ridin' for?"

"Chisum."

"So. Then here's yore pay," the murderer said pleasantly and shot the unsuspecting cowboy through the head.

There is another story, which goes back to an earlier period of his life. This bears some of the earmarks of legend, which has grown about the name of Billy the Kid to such an extent that it is hard to know what is true. Also, this story seems to me to parallel too closely the experience of Charlie Wall. It was told me by an officer of the court at Mesilla.

With Jesse Evans, Billy Morton, and Frank Baker (two of whom he later killed) Billy came upon three Mexicans busy turning water into their ditches from a canal. Billy and his friends were full of the devil and bad whisky.

"Watch me make 'em kick," Billy said.

Thereupon he killed the three Mexicans and nearly precipitated a race war. I give this as an example of the sort of story, usually not authenticated, which has grown up with the passage of years. According to Siringo, in his history of the Kid, Charlie Wall got into a quarrel with Mexicans over the irrigating of his land and killed four of them before the guns stopped roaring. He fled to Lincoln and was in jail there at the time Billy the Kid killed Bell and Ollinger. There has been, perhaps, some juggling of the memory which confused Wall and the young outlaw.

There is nothing legendary about the next killings I mention. Billy shot down a bad man from Texas named Grant at Fort Sumner. Later he slew, without any semblance of excuse, Jim Carlyle, a law officer who trusted the Kid by going into his camp with a white flag to offer him terms of surrender. Carlyle was with a posse from White Oaks which had the outlaw gang cornered at the Greathouse ranch. He knew Billy in a rather casual friendly way and said he was sure young Bonney would not hurt him. The Kid kept him a prisoner for hours under constant threats of death. The generally accepted story is that Carlyle, believing the outlaws meant to murder him, made a break to escape by diving through a window. Billy's first shot brought him down outside the house, the second finished him as he tried to crawl away, a badly wounded man.

But the young terror of New Mexico was drawing near the end of his rope. The country had had enough of him. It elected Pat Garrett sheriff of Lincoln County, on the platform that he was to break up the gang of rustlers and murderers terrorizing the settlers. The Canadian River Cattle Association appointed John W. Poe its representative to co-operate with the authorities in New Mexico in suppressing the stock raiders. These two men were responsible for ending the career of Billy the Kid. They were from the Panhandle, both of them, and so were most of the assistants who worked with them to trail down the gang of Billy the Kid.

Pat Garrett was a long lean man, six foot plus several inches. More than any other factor he was the instrument in bringing back law to Lincoln County. A great deal of sentiment has been wasted on this young murderer Bonney, but the plain truth is that he had gone bad and was as much a menace to the community as a mad dog. Garrett and the men who tracked him down were law bringers, as Rhodes and Bechdolt have said. They were game fighting men who took their lives in their hands to bring to justice the outlaws, and it is to be noted that they did their best to capture rather than kill Billy and his gang.

Word came to Garrett that Billy and his gang would be at Fort Sumner for a dance a few days before Christmas. The sheriff and his posse got to saddle at once. The men riding with Garrett were cowboys who had come up from Texas to try to stop the stealing of cattle by Billy the Kid's gang. Charley Siringo had loaned him Jim East, Lon Chambers, and Lee Hall. Emory, Williams, and Bozeman were from another posse of Lone Star state riders. Barney Mason, related to Garrett by marriage, had brought the news to the sheriff and rode back to Fort Sumner with him.

Garrett waited for the outlaws to show up. Chambers, on guard, ran in to say that the Kid's gang was riding up. Six shadows loomed out of the darkness, grew more definite. They rode straight toward the officers.

"Throw up your hands," called Garrett.

The foremost rider, Tom O'Folliard, dragged at the bridle and reached for his weapon. There came the roar of guns. Tom Pickett, Billy Wilson, Charlie Bowdre, Dave Rudabaugh, and the Kid wheeled their horses and dashed away. O'Folliard, shot to death, sank down in the road and died in a short time.

Next morning Garrett took up the trail. There had been a heavy snow and there could be no tracking. But a ranchman gave information that the outlaws had headed for Stinking Spring. There was a small rock house there. The posse waited outside in the snow till morning.

Out of the house came Charlie Bowdre to feed the horses. Garrett called to him to surrender. The man reached for his six-shooter and was shot down at once by Garrett and Lee Hall. He staggered back into the house. Jim East heard the Kid say, "Charlie, you're done for. Go out and get one of 'em before you die."

Bowdre stumbled out, gun in hand. He could not

shoot, and none of the posse attempted to do so. Garrett drew his posse around the house so that escape was impossible. A horse stationed outside was shot in such a way that it blocked the doorway. Thus two horses that had been taken into the house could not be used for a getaway.

Garrett crept up an arroyo and opened a parley. The Kid declined to surrender. Bowdre died. The siege dragged on. The posse ate food and drank hot coffee. The besieged did neither. At last the outlaws surrendered on promise of safe-conduct to prison.

The prisoners were taken to Las Vegas and a mob gathered to lynch them. The resentment was principally against Rudabaugh because he had recently killed a Vegas man, but it included all the outlaws. The crowd swarmed around the train, which was ready to leave for Santa Fe.

There were three guards, for the sheriff had brought East and Emory with him. Pat left the other two with the prisoners and stepped out upon the platform. It was a ticklish moment. He looked down upon a hundred furious faces, most of them Mexican.

"We want Rudabaugh. We want the Kid," they shouted.

"Can't have either of 'em," Garrett answered, hard eyes travelling from one to another. "Better go home, boys, for if you rush this car I'll sure give Billy and his friends guns."

An Easterner who chanced to be present wrote an account of the affair for one of the great New York magazines not long afterward. The crowd surged forward, cursed, shouted, roared with rage. But that one intrepid man on the platform stood between them and their prey. If for a moment he had weakened they would have dragged their victims to death. Garrett held them for more than an hour, until at last the train began to move and the danger was past.

Rudabaugh was tried, convicted, sentenced to be hanged; he escaped from prison and was not heard from again. Exactly the same sequence of events occurred in the case of his chief. Billy was taken to Lincoln to be executed.

The days slipped away. Garrett and his prisoner were friendly enough. One of the jailors, J. W. Bell, treated Billy with consideration. The other, Bob Ollinger, never missed a chance to revile the condemned man.

The outlaw was quartered in the courthouse, which formerly had been the Murphy store and to-day is a school building. He was shackled hand and foot. Bell felt sorry for him and sometimes played cards with him. They were so engaged one day while Garrett was out of town and Ollinger was at dinner at the hotel opposite. No man knows how it happened, but somehow Billy got Bell's revolver and killed him as the deputy turned to fly down the stairway.

Ollinger heard the sound of the shot perhaps and gave it little weight. But he started across the road to investigate.

A voice from the window above hailed him. "Hello, Bob!"

He looked up. That smiling devil Billy the Kid was

looking down at him, a double-barrelled shotgun in his hands.

The gun roared and Ollinger fell dead.

Billy had very small hands and wrists. He slipped off his cuffs, shuffled to an adjoining room where the weapons were kept, and helped himself liberally. He forced a man to file away the chain which bound his legs together, then danced a jig on the little porch while a horse was being saddled for him. Lincoln stood and watched the performance without a word of protest.

The Kid mounted, heavily encumbered with weapons, was thrown by the bronc, jumped warily to his feet, climbed to the saddle again, and rode away. This was at least two hours after the double killing.

John W. Poe, later a banker at Roswell, New Mexico, joined Garrett in the hunt for the escaped bandit. It was generally believed that he had gone to Mexico. This would be the reasonable thing for him to do. But rumours persisted that he was still hiding in the chaparral of Lincoln County.

In 1918 I talked with John W. Poe at his home in Roswell, New Mexico. He told me then the story of the death of Billy the Kid. He was a quiet man, reserved, not given to talk. He told me that he had very seldom talked about the affair. Next year, while I was in the Panhandle at his famous ranch, Mr. Charles Goodnight showed me a letter from Poe, with which was inclosed a typewritten account of the death of Billy the Kid. It had been dictated the day after I was with him. Later Poe detailed the story more at length to E. A. Brininstool and it has been printed by him in a pamphlet.

Both Garrett and Poe scoured the country, but neither of them got any definite information about the Kid. Both of them felt that he had left New Mexico. Several months passed.

Poe had been marshal at Tascosa before coming to New Mexico, and that alone is almost a certificate of efficiency as a peace officer. For Tascosa was a wild and woolly town. He stood six foot in his stockings, a man among a thousand, game, determined, resourceful. Billy the Kid was up against two of the best men in the territory.

To Poe, who was staying at White Oaks, came George Graham with a story which might or might not be true. While sleeping in the hay at a livery stable, Graham had heard friends of the Kid say that he was at Fort Sumner. Poe doubted this, and talked it over with Garrett. Neither of them believed, but neither was willing to ignore a possible clew. They took with them a deputy named McKinney, and the three men rode to a point near Fort Sumner. They camped there for the night.

Garrett and McKinney were both known at Ft. Sumner; Poe was not. Next day the Tascosa man rode in to look the ground over. His presence was noted at once, for the village was small. Poe gave it out that he was a White Oaks miner. He hung around for hours but learned nothing. Yet the actions of the villagers and of a rancher whom he met later impressed upon him a feeling that the Kid was not far away.

Toward evening Poe met his two companions at an appointed place. They talked the situation over and hid in a peach orchard on the edge of the town. It seemed to Garrett that they were on a wild-goose chase, and he said so. Poe suggested Garrett talk with Pete Maxwell before they leave. This man was the son of the grantee who had received the famous Maxwell land grant. He was a man of local influence, though he possessed no such wealth as his father had once commanded. Billy the Kid was a friend of his sister, and it was sure that Pete would know if he was here.

The three men walked to the Maxwell house, a long adobe building which had formerly been the headquarters of United States officers when troops had been stationed here. The end room was the one used by Maxwell.

Garrett left the other two men standing outside while he went in to see Maxwell. Poe and McKinney sat down and made themselves comfortable. Neither of them had any idea how hot a trail they had struck.

They had hardly seated themselves when a young fellow, bareheaded and barefooted, walked lightly along the long porch toward them. He was almost upon Poe before he caught sight of the two men. Then, startled, he leaped back. A revolver flashed to light.

"*Quien es ? Quien es ?*" he demanded tensely.

It did not occur to Poe that this was the man he

had hunted so long. Nor did the Kid think for a moment that these men were officers seeking him. But it was his business to guard himself against every stranger. Again he called out that sharp *"Quien es ?"* ("Who is it?")

Poe rose and moved toward him, telling him not to be alarmed, that nobody was going to hurt him. What passed through the mind of the Kid nobody knows. He was disturbed at the presence of these men, but now that he was a fugitive, dependent on his friends for hospitality and safety, he did not want to kill *their* friends recklessly. So he backed into the doorway of Maxwell's room and vanished from Poe's sight.

Garrett had found Pete Maxwell lying in the darkness on his bed. He had just started to speak with Maxwell when he heard the voices outside. He crouched lower, listening.

A moment later someone came into the room and moved forward toward Maxwell's bed. "Who are those fellows outside, Pete?" he asked. He caught sight of Garrett's shadowy form and stepped back. Again that sharp *"Quien es ?"* rang out. Garrett fired from where he sat. Billy the Kid fell dead.

This was about midnight, July 14, 1881. Next day an inquest was held and the body was buried beside those of Tom O'Folliard and Charlie Bowdre, both of whom had previously been killed by Garrett.

Law had come into the mesquite.

Just as in the case of Jesse James, persistent stories were circulated to the effect that the Kid had not been killed. Both George and Frank Coe believed, at least until recent years, that Billy was still alive in Mexico.

George Coe said to me, sawing the air with the hand from which Buckshot Roberts's bullet had looped a finger, "Garrett was his friend, had gone to dances with him at Fort Sumner and frolicked with him. Why would he shoot him? No, sir. He helped Billy out of the country. That's what he did."

The Coes were wrong. The story of Billy the Kid's death and the manner of it are as well authenticated as any historical fact we have. A dozen men saw his dead body who knew him as well as they would have known their own brother.

In St. Joseph, Missouri, within the past few years I met men who believe that Jesse James is still living. Half a dozen men in recent times have been picked out and exploited as Quantrell the raider. You will hear in Arizona old-timers say the Apache Kid was not killed at the time he disappeared. A great number of people in Europe believed persistently that one of the daughters of the Czar was living in Germany. Englishmen will tell you even now that Kitchener was not lost at sea but taken prisoner. These myths usually have their foundations in rumours based on hope.

Few of the actors in the Lincoln County drama are still alive. Of those mentioned in this article more than fifty came to violent deaths. Even the baby with whom Billy the Kid played at Dowlan's Mill had a tragic end. Pioneer days in Cattleland were turbulent ones.

But in passing judgment times and conditions must be considered. These men were as varied as you and I and our next-door neighbour. Many were honest and honourable and God-fearing. Others were a blend of good and bad, wild young hellions given to bad whisky and generous impulses. The worst of them could do a fine thing on occasion. The best was no saint but a man driven at times to make a choice of evils.

Nearly all of them were strong—and game. Good or bad, there was one essential acid test all must meet. Sooner or later the day came when the frontier assayed each soul in the crucible of danger. Then men watched to see the result. Would a man go through? Did he have sand in his craw, what hard men denominate roughly "guts"? If not, the frontier had no use for him. If he went his way quietly minding his own business he was negligible. He was perhaps good enough to reach eminence in the soft life of cities where at any time he can appeal to the law for protection. But he had no chance for leadership in the hard-riding, fighting West.

I have heard cowboys murmur a bit of doggerel that is applicable to outlaws and the men who hunted them:

> Never was a horse that couldn't be rode,
> Never was a horse that couldn't be throwed.

There was never a killer so deadly with a gun that game men, acting for the law, would not dispute the right of way with him. Billy the Kid was a wonderful shot, probably better with the six-shooter than Garrett, but when it came to a test of strength the lank puncher from the Panhandle was a better man. He had the staying qualities which counted in a long campaign.

Garrett, now a national figure, broke up a bad gang of rustlers and retired to ranching. But there was need of men who could tame bad men. He was forced into the harness again. In Wheeler County, Texas, he commanded a company of Rangers. Three times he was sheriff of Donna Ana County, New Mexico. In 1901 Mr. Roosevelt appointed him collector of customs at El Paso. It is said that Garrett failed of a reappointment because of a singular lapse. At a reunion of the Rough Riders in San Antonio he was invited to lunch with the President and took along as a guest his friend Tom Powers. Not till later did Mr. Roosevelt learn that Powers was a saloon keeper.

At the time of his death Garrett was ranching. The manner of his taking off is a curious fulfilment of the scriptural prophecy that he who takes the sword shall perish by the sword. He was killed over a trifling matter, February 29, 1908, by an unknown youth, Wayne Brazel.

That is the story generally accepted by the public. It has the backing of a legal investigation and the admission of Brazel that it is true. But many of those "in the know" believe that Pat Garrett was killed by a murderer who answered to the name of Miller. This desperado was a killer of the worst type. On one occasion he shot down a man and then slew the witnesses to the killing. (It is pleasant to be able to record that a vigilance committee terminated the career of Miller, together with three of his associates, by hanging them to the rafters of a stable, at Ada, Oklahoma.)

THE "APACHE KID"

One of the Worst of the Indian Renegades of the Old West

THE two most feared bad Indians that the Southwest has known were Geronimo and the "Apache Kid." The latter typified all the evil traits of a tribe notorious for diabolical outrage and unrestrained savagery. For years the mention of his name in Arizona or Sonora carried a shiver with it. He was the last and the worst of that renegade band of Mescalero Apaches who left a red trail of blood behind them as they swept across the desert. To-day southern Arizona and northern Sonora are dotted with crosses which cover the graves of victims of this ferocious renegade. He was distinguished for cruelty even among a people who bear the palm for refinement of torture.

The "Apache Kid" was brought up at the San Carlos Agency under the eye of Al Sieber, the famous chief of scouts. As a lad he flitted in and out of the fort unnoticed. He was just "the kid," in no wise to be noted more than any other little brown-bodied, long-haired, impassive Indian youth. As he grew up he developed unusual ability as a trailer. Sieber noticed this and employed him as an army scout. Gradually he advanced the boy until he became a first sergeant of the Apache government scouts.

Chief Toga-de-chuz, a San Carlos Apache, was the father of the Kid. Forty years before he and another young buck known as "Rip" fell out over an Indian girl. Toga-de-chuz married her and made mock of his rival. A white man fights or forgets. Rip was an Apache. He did neither. He waited forty years for his chance, and then knifed his enemy at a big dance on the Gila. The Indians present were sodden drunk at the time. Nobody could prove that "Rip" had done it. But he and his horse were both missing in the morning.

The Kid was the oldest son of Toga-de-chuz. It therefore fell to him to avenge his father's death. But he had plenty of time—and like Rip he sat down and waited the opportunity. Sieber warned him that there must be no killing, but the lad said nothing either good or bad.

Not long afterward Sieber, with Captain Pierce, the Indian agent, rode over to Camp Apache to distribute some money to the natives there. The Kid was left at the agency as chief in command. He very promptly selected five of his men, rode over to the Aravaipo River, and murdered old Rip.

The Kid and his assistants deserted the service at once and rejoined their people in camp. Sieber sent word to them to come down to the agency. The Kid went, accompanied by a band of ten bucks. They drew rein in front of Sieber's tent.

The scout stepped out. He detected latent rebellion, but ignored it, as a soldier must often do. His cool eye ranged over the band and stopped at the Apache Kid.

"Get off that horse," commanded Sieber.

The young man slid to the ground.

"Disarm those men."

The Kid took their rifles from them.

"Take them to the guardhouse."

The young Indian still had the last gun in his hand. He raised it and fired at the scout. Sieber leaped back into his tent for his rifle. When he reappeared a moment later the Apaches poured a volley at him, wounding him in the leg and shattering it. Sieber fell, coolly took aim, and shot a renegade through the heart. The rest fled. From that day the Apache Kid was an outlaw.

At this time Tom Horn, famous through the West in turn as a scout, cowboy, army pack master, and cattle detective, was working a mine on the Aravaipo.

Tom was a Westerner of the old school. He had many good qualities, but he was later hanged in Wyoming for killing a boy in cold blood. He had been hired by cattlemen to stop rustling, and this was his method.

One day he went out to catch his horse, which he had turned loose to graze up the cañon, and he noticed the track of a moccasin covering the trail of the dragging rope attached to his pony. Horn followed the trail till it merged in the tracks of several other horses. They were all headed south. It was the

Apache Kid and his fellow renegades making for Sonora. Horn got another horse, rode over to the agency thirty miles away, and learned what had happened.

Meanwhile, the Apache renegades crossed the ridge to Table Mountain. They stampeded and stole a bunch of horses from the Atchley Ranch, swooped down on the cabin of "Wallapai" Clarke when he was away and murdered his partner, Bill Diehl, then pushed up into the San Pedro country. They followed the course of the Sonoita, tortured and killed a rancher named Mike Grace en route, and a few miles from there were headed north by Uncle Sam's cavalry. In the Rincon Mountains the pursuers under Lieutenant Johnson came up with them. In a running fight two of the Apaches were killed and the rest dismounted. Tom Horn's horse was captured with others and returned to him.

This was the beginning of this young Indian's nefarious career. From now on every white man was his enemy. His own people looked upon him as a scourge and feared him. He had but to demand the best horses of the tribe and they were his. If his eyes coveted a squaw he took her whether she would or not. He proved to be so wily, so desperate, and so utterly merciless that gradually his fellow renegades deserted him. Victoria, Cochise, and Geronimo had always gone on the warpath at the head of a bunch of Apache braves, but the Kid worked his devilish mischief alone unless it might be for some poor unwilling squaw who by chance was his prisoner.

In the rough uplands of the Rincon, the Mescal, and the Catalina Mountains, as well as in the sun-baked cactus plains between, the renegade roved on his bloody missions. He would swoop down on the lonely freighter from the brush where he lay hidden, or would shoot from cover the hardy prospector in the Galluros who dared to operate within striking distance of him. An adept equally at covering his own trail and at following that of others, the mesquite and the chaparral afforded him excellent cover. A tireless rider, a crack shot, shielded by his tribesmen who yet hated him, inured from childhood to the torrid heat of summer and the cold of the mountain winters, the young desperado was able for years to defy his pursuers.

His audacity was so great that he would venture almost under the guns of the frontier forts. He and one of his comrades on one occasion slipped into the San Carlos reservation and induced two women of the tribe to accompany them back into the mountains. The officer in charge called to him one of his best Indian scouts, known as Josh, and ordered him to take the trail. He was to run down the renegades or lose his position as sergeant of scouts.

Josh disappeared. Months passed, but no word came from him. One day he slipped into the fort and appeared before the officer who had sent him on his mission. The colonel looked up. Josh, impassive as a sphinx, stood before him. He carried in one hand something wrapped in a blanket.

"Well?" demanded the officer.

Josh deftly unrolled his blanket so as to throw its contents on the table. The astonished officer leaped to his feet with an exclamation. There stared at him the head of an Indian—the head of the Apache Kid's companion in deviltry, with its black, coarse hair, its cruel, thin lips, its swarthy look of savagery present even in death.

The life of the squaw whom the Kid captured was a pitiable one. Forced to move continually from place to place in order to escape capture, her existence was one of continual hardship that only the hardiest frame could endure. Fortunately for her the Kid's San Carlos squaw was as active and strong as a man. She soon wearied of her treacherous husband and became afraid of him, for she knew that if ever she hampered his movements he would kill her without compunction. Several times she tried to escape, but did not succeed. He watched her like a lynx, hobbled her at night like a horse, and when he was about to set out on one of his murderous expeditions tied her to a tree till his return. For months she trailed across mountains and deserts with him before she finally succeeded in escaping.

The Kid got tired of the hardships of his life. He decided that he wanted to be a good Indian, who only killed men occasionally. He returned to the reservation, where he lay hidden. To vary the monotony he killed a freighter one day while he was there in hiding. Then, after some negotiations, he gave himself up to the government. He was tried for one of his crimes, condemned to a long term in prison by the federal courts, and was soon afterward pardoned by President Cleveland.

He was at once arrested again by Glenn Reynolds, sheriff of Gila County, Arizona. The Kid was tried along with five other Indians for the killing of the freighter at Twelve Mile Pole on the San Carlos River. They were all condemned to a life sentence at Yuma, the territorial penitentiary.

Glenn Reynolds was a typical product of Arizona. He was lithe, active, rather tall and very strong. One of the best shots in the whole Southwest, he was absolutely fearless, as he had shown on numberless occasions in dealing both with Indians and bad men. In a land where men are quick on the trigger, Glenn Reynolds commanded unusual respect for his nerve and skill. Tom Horn was his deputy, another man conspicuous for his splendid physique, cool daring, and knowledge of frontier conditions.

But just now Horn, who was the champion roper of Arizona, was unfortunately absent at a steer-tying contest in Phœnix. The prisoners had to be taken from Globe to Florence by stage over one of the wildest regions of the West. That road is now a part of what is known as the Apache trail and is traversed in comfortable buses by thousands of tourists. It is one of the scenic highways of the country. Rugged mountains, deep cañons, narrow gorges, and cactus deserts had to be crossed—and on the way unruly bands of Apaches might attempt a rescue. There was without doubt need of a strong guard. But Reynolds had found trouble on previous occasions in collecting from the county money he had personally expended in employing assistant guards to take criminals to the penitentiary. He was quick to resent any imputation of being too careful of his own skin. He was proud of his record and would rather take a chance than seem too cautious. He had fought and trailed Apaches, so he understood their ways. It was a common saying that Glenn Reynolds was a match for Indian treachery.

Reynolds decided to take one deputy with him to Yuma to guard the Apaches. He regretted deeply the absence of Horn, but selected "Hunky Dory" Holmes, a rollicking, happy-go-lucky fellow of undoubted courage, to go with him on the journey.

Holmes carried a Winchester, Reynolds a double-barrelled shotgun loaded with buckshot. Each had in addition a 45-calibre Colt's revolver. The six Indians were handcuffed and shackled in pairs, each of the Indians having one wrist and one ankle chained to the wrist and ankle of a companion.

The party took the stage at Globe on November 1, 1892. Great care was exercised in watching the Apaches, for each of the six had a bad record. They sat sullenly, saying little to each other. That the Apache Kid was their leader Reynolds saw at once. There was a Mexican prisoner along, too, but he was a mere incident.

All day the stage went up and down sandy washes and across mountains. The party camped that night on the banks of the Gila. After supper prisoners and guards sat around the camp fires and smoked, though Holmes, Reynolds, and Gene Livingston, the stage driver, nursed their guns rather closely. One by one the renegades fell asleep. Livingston presently rolled up in a blanket and dropped into slumber. But "Hunky Dory" and Glenn Reynolds sat the night through by the camp fire with their guns across their knees. They were taking no chances, they told Livingston.

The morning broke cold, cloudy, and dismal, but with the coming of dawn the strain on the officers lifted. They were past the worst now. The probability of an attempt at rescue began to grow less. After breakfast the stage was loaded again. It continued to creep up and rattle down the Arizona hills as it followed the course of the river road. After an abrupt rise the stage road from Globe to Casa Grande drops into a narrow valley, crosses the Gila, and winds up a very steep sand wash.

The sand was so deep that the horses could hardly drag the heavy stage up the long hill. It was like Reynolds to suggest that the prisoners and their guard would walk up the incline to save the horses. The Apache Kid was freed from his companion, so that Holmes and Reynolds could each take charge of three of the Indians. The Mexican was left handcuffed inside the stage.

Because the morning was chilly, Reynolds and Holmes each wore heavy overcoats buttoned to the neck. Their revolvers were in belts inside of these, but

Reynolds carried his shotgun under his arm and Holmes his Winchester. The Indians had been more talkative this morning, but neither of the officers understood their gibberish. It was exceedingly unfortunate that Tom Horn, who knew their language like a book, was not present.

Somehow Holmes and his detachment got some distance ahead of Reynolds, who stepped in front of his prisoners to call Holmes to go slower. As the sheriff passed him, the Apache Kid with a whoop leaped on him like a panther. His heavy handcuffs crashed down on the officer's forehead, then slipped over his head and down his body. Reynolds flung the lithe Indian about like a child as he struggled. But the handcuffs about his body held down and pinioned his arms.

At the sound of the first Apache war whoop the Indians with Holmes flung themselves on him, wrested the rifle from him, threw him down and killed him. Then they ran back with his rifle to help their comrades.

Reynolds was still fighting desperately. He had succeeded in freeing his arms and was struggling for possession of the rifle. His revolvers were buried hopelessly beneath his overcoat, which was still belted down by the Apache Kid's handcuffed arms about his waist. The Indians that had murdered Holmes now beat the sheriff down with their iron handcuffs and killed him with Holmes's rifle.

At the first shot Livingston leaned out of the stage to see what was going on. It was immediately plain to him that there was no chance of saving

Reynolds, and Holmes was already dead. As he hesitated, one of the Indians fired at him. The ball struck him in the cheek, just missed the spinal cord, and passed out at the back of the neck. Livingston fell forward into the boot of the stage, and the frightened horses galloped away in a wild run. Livingston was jolted to the ground. The Mexican stopped them, cut loose one of the horses, and mounted. The Indians fired at him. Twice the horse threw him, but the third time he mounted the Mexican stuck to his place and escaped. He hastened to Florence and gave the alarm.

Meanwhile, the Apache Kid searched the body of Reynolds, found his keys, and unlocked their irons. They hurriedly stripped the dead bodies of valuables and decamped. Seeing Livingston's wound they had supposed him dead. After the Apaches left he dragged himself back to Riverside and gave the alarm. A posse took the field in pursuit. But the wily Kid eluded his enemies till a storm broke and wiped out the trail.

Six months later the five companions of the Kid were captured. They were tried and condemned. The time approached for their execution, and the death watch sat within six feet of them day in and day out. On the night before the day set for the execution the Apaches apparently went to sleep as serenely as if they still had forty years of life before them. In the morning the death watch discovered that three of them had taken off their breechcloths and strangled themselves without a sound. The other two had lain in front of them and shielded them from the eyes of the guards. These last two were hanged six hours later.

But the Kid, the worst of them all, was still out. Near Camp Grant he swooped down on a prairie schooner. A woman had just sold her ranch and was on her way with her boy and baby to meet her husband. The renegade shot her in cold blood and then killed the boy. The baby for some reason he spared.

The old army scout, Dupont, told me that soon after this he met the outlaw on a trail in the Catalinas face to face. He had known the young Apache since he was a child, so that he recognized him at once. Both men were armed with old single-shot rifles. Neither one cared to risk his life on one shot, for if he should not kill he would be at the mercy of the other. Each stood alertly with his gun half raised, neither speaking a word. They watched each other steadily, then backed away and found seats on boulders. From noon till nearly sunset the two men sat there facing each other. Then the Apache rose. "Me going," he grunted, beginning to back cautiously away. As soon as he had turned a bend in the trail Dupont "lit a shuck" for home, as he himself phrased it.

Another well-known army scout, Wallapai Clarke, had a feud with this outlaw that endured for years. It is still an open question whether the Kid came to his death at the hands of Clarke.

Bill Diehl had been a partner of Clarke, and when the outlaw murdered him, the army scout swore vengeance on him. John Scanlon, a third partner, had just left the Clarke cabin to cut some mesquite for firewood when he heard a couple of shots. Running back to the cabin, he found Diehl lying dead in a pool of blood just outside the door. Scanlon barricaded himself in and opened fire. The Indians retreated, taking with them Clarke's favourite horse, Old Pete.

Two years later Scanlon and Clarke left the cabin on their mining claim in charge of a young Englishman named Mercer while they went to Tucson after chuck. Clarke advised Mercer not to leave the cabin without his rifle, but the latter scouted the idea of danger. He went out next morning to take his morning bath in the creek near by. His little dog barked, and he heard a twig snap. Remembering Clarke's warning, he fled for the house in a whine of bullets. He had only time to bolt the door when the Indians rushed forward. The Kid led them, but the Englishman held them off till the return of Clarke and Scanlon.

The Indians drew back into the brush. That night Clarke slipped out of the cabin and stole down to the corral below. He wanted to make sure that the horses were safe. Suddenly the scout saw something move on the other side of the arroyo. The moon was up, and he recognized Old Pete. An Indian was leading him and another one followed at his heels. Clarke fired instantly. The first Indian toppled over. He fired again. The second instantly disappeared. Next day Clarke crossed the arroyo. He found the body of a squaw whom he had killed by mistake. A trail of blood showed where her master, the Kid, had gone. For a time the white man followed them. They disappeared among the rocks.

From that time the Apache Kid travelled on his raids no more. Whether he died from wounds at the hands of Hualpai Clarke or was a victim of consumption has never been made clear. But no more burned cabins and bleaching bones marked the trails which he had been used to follow. Somewhere in the mountain passes of southern Arizona his own bones lie unburied as those of many of his victims have done.

THE STORY OF BEECHER'S ISLAND

How Fifty American Frontier Scouts Held Back Thousands of Cheyenne and Sioux Indians for Nine Days

EXCEPT Custer's last fight, there is no tale of Indian border warfare between the troopers and the natives more thrilling than that of the gallant stand of Forsyth's scouts at Beecher's Island, on the Arikaree River, in Colorado. The writer was told the tale by George Oakes, one of the survivors, then living at Tucson, Arizona, but long since dead. He sets it down substantially as it was narrated to him. There were no heroics in the story as Oakes told it. For Oakes was an old-timer, an Indian fighter and buffalo hunter. This expedition was all in the day's work for him.

It became apparent early in 1868 that the frontier Indians were about to take the warpath. During the last six months of that year, they murdered more than one hundred and fifty settlers and freighters, besides destroying a great deal of valuable property.

General George A. Forsyth, then a young brevet colonel who had won his spurs by distinguished gallantry during the Civil War, was appointed, at his own request, to the command of a body of fifty scouts which he was authorized by General Sheridan to enroll and equip. This he did at Fort Harker and Fort Hayes, and immediately took the field with his command. Both the morale and equipment of these men were of the best. They were frontiersmen inured to hardship, excellent marksmen, and well used to Indian methods of warfare. Among them were First Lieutenant Fred H. Beecher, a nephew of the great preacher, Henry Ward Beecher; General William H. H. McCall, who won his star on account of distinguished and brilliant work during the Civil War, but who, by reason of his great desire to see active service, was serving as sergeant in this little body of troopers; Abner Grover, chief of scouts, commonly called "Sharp" Grover, a grizzled frontiersman who knew every turn of Western life; and many other well-known characters of the border.

The troops advanced across the Saline and the south fork of the Solomon, then moved up Beaver Creek toward Fort Wallace. Here word came in from Sheridan, a little town which was then the terminus of the Kansas Pacific Railroad, that Indians had raided a freighting outfit and killed some of the teamsters. Forsyth made at once for the spot of the catastrophe. This reached, the trail of the Indians was followed for a time and then lost. But Colonel Forsyth pushed on toward the Indian country until his command reached the Arikaree Fork of the Republican River. The trail had by this time been picked up again, and presently broadened into a travelled road.

It became apparent that the party was approaching a large Indian encampment, and several of the men felt that it would be wise to turn back. But the commanding officer said he had been sent out to fight Indians and he proposed to fight them. The scouts encamped that night in a little valley on the banks of the stream.

Opposite them was an island—afterward named Beecher's Island in memory of the gallant young officer who lost his life on it—lying in the wide sandy bed of the stream about seventy-five yards from each shore. Like all rivers of the arid lands, Arikaree fork in the spring is a torrent, and late in summer is a mere brook which an active man can leap across or can wade through without the water reaching much above his boot-tops. Near the middle of the island was a thicket of alders, and at its lower extremity several young cottonwood trees. On one side of the island the land sloped gradually down to the river, while on the other bank the rise was scarcely perceptible.

That night the party camped on the banks of the stream, the men taking watch and watch about. It fell cold, and the men lay in pairs under the same blankets for the sake of warmth. Colonel Forsyth and Lieutenant Beecher bunked together within an arm's length of George Oakes, whose "bunkie" was Jack Hurst. Oakes had the first watch of the night and about two o'clock waked Hurst to take his turn on picket guard. Before Oakes tumbled over to sleep he said to his bunkie:

"Jack, watch that horse of mine. It may break away, for it won't stand picketed. If it does, drive it back."

"All right," returned Hurst, and the next minute Oakes was sound asleep. He was awakened three hours later by hearing a man say, "Oakes' horse is straying too far."

Hurst drove the bronco back and tied it to the projecting root of a dead cottonwood, but Oakes, thoroughly awakened, threw off his blankets and got up. The first faint streaks of daylight were just breaking at this time. Suddenly someone cried out, "A herd of buffaloes is coming right into camp, boys." A moment later Colonel Forsyth's voice rang out like a bugle: "Indians! Turn out! Turn out!"

The land lay a rolling plain, and above one of the rises thirteen Indians could be seen silhouetted against the sky-line. Presently they were lost in the dip, but emerged again at the next rise. In an instant the silent camp awakened to bustling life. Apparently all was confusion, but in reality everyone was busy packing the camp equipments. Everything but the mule, which carried the doctor's medicine case, was packed, and before this had been attended to the Indians were upon them whooping and shooting. Plainly this was an attempt to stampede the horses, but by good fortune it had failed, though so close had it been to success that several horses were captured in the rush. The horse of Oakes tore up its picket pin and broke right through the other horses. He caught hold of the rope and was dragged over the ground, but succeeded in hanging to it. Seven or eight of the troopers scattered through the long buffalo grass and began to shoot at the Indians, killing one of them and two of their horses.

Saddles were slapped on in a hurry, and the little troop started up from the river bank, for they realized that a large body of Indians must be close at hand to warrant such a bold attempt at a stampede. Presently the soldiers topped the first rise and came upon a sight none of them will ever forget.

More than five hundred Cheyennes and Brulé-Sioux faced them on horseback in the prettiest line of battle conceivable. A deep murmur of dismay and admiration ran through the ranks of the scouts. From every clump of mesquite, from every wash and hollow, from out of the sagebrush and the chaparral, poured the shouting natives toward the little body of doomed troopers. On horseback, afoot, armed with bows and arrows and long needle guns secured by them at the massacre of Fort Kearny, they leaped triumphantly forward. The men stood beside their horses and poured lead from their repeating Spencers into the advancing horde. Colonel Forsyth's first impulse was to take and hold the hill, but he at once saw that this was not feasible, and the command fell back to the river bank. A hundred yards below them was the place where they had watered their horses on the previous evening. Here there was a sloping bank so that the animals could get down into the dry bed of the stream, but where they were forced now to take the bank it was sheer and precipitous. The men stood huddled at the river's edge, some of them kicking away the bank with their toes while others held back the attacking natives. So closely did the Indians press them that scarcely twenty feet separated the defenders and the assailants. The Cheyennes and the Sioux circled round and round them, screaming out their war cries and pouring on them a hail of bullets and arrows. At this point many of the horses were killed because they were so closely packed. As the men broke down the bank with their horses and made toward the island, Beecher, Grover, McCall, and Colonel Forsyth himself were conspicuous for the steadiness and gallantry with which they held back the enemy. Colonel Forsyth stood with a six-shooter in each hand and emptied them as coolly as if he were practising at a mark.

For a few minutes it was touch and go at the river's bank, but the rear guard held back the swarms of natives while the other troopers and their horses slithered down the banks into the dry bed of the stream. Fighting desperately, they won their way to the water, forded the stream, and took possession of the little island. Half a dozen of the men dropped into the long grass and with their deadly rifles made good the retreat of their comrades. Behind a drooping cottonwood John Lyden and George Oakes took shelter. The Indians began to close in on them. "It's pretty hot here. We'd better take shelter behind our horses, Oakes," said Lyden. They did so, and a moment later the cottonwood was shot clean through. At this point the Indians lay in the bear grass scarce a dozen yards from the outlying scouts, but luckily the majority of the troopers managed to reach the island in safety.

The Indians, realizing their error in not having occupied the island, now made a furious assault upon it. From all sides they converged toward it and poured in a deadly fire. Stealthily working through the long grass, hundreds of picked warriors galled the troopers with a steady fire. Perhaps the deadliest execution of the siege occurred then. The horses were shot down by scores, and more than one brave frontiersman went to meet his last account. Colonel Forsyth, exposing himself fearlessly to keep his men steady, stood up in full sight of the Cheyennes despite the warning of his fellow officers.

Meanwhile, part of the men began to throw up rough fortifications, while the rest of them held back the enemy. With knives and tin eating plates they scooped out of the sand holes large enough to protect a man's body. As a further protection dead horses were dragged in front of the rifle pits. At this juncture Colonel Forsyth was badly wounded in the leg. Dr. Mooers, who had been doing deadly execution with his rifle and who had given a splendid exhibition of fearlessness, was struck by a bullet in the forehead, just after having killed an Indian. The ball went through his brain and he was never conscious again, though he lived for several days. A trooper named Burke scooped in the sand a little well, and during the next night an S-shaped trench was run so that the men could communicate with their water supply and with each other without exposing themselves to the fire of the enemy. But fatalities continued to occur at intervals, and many of the men were seriously wounded. Colonel Forsyth was struck again. Oakes had the tip of his ear shot off, and shortly after was hit more seriously. Young Farley, shot in the chest, had his arm bound up and continued to shoot with his left hand. His father, fatally wounded, continued to load and fire with unerring coolness almost to the end. Sergeant McCall and a dozen of the scouts scarce mentioned their wounds until night-fall had put an end to the day's fighting. A curious accident was that which occurred to a young school-teacher named Frank Harrington. An Indian arrow struck him in the head. He pulled out the arrow, but the socket remained firm in the bone joint. Soon afterward a bullet ploughed the socket out. He bound his head with a handkerchief and continued to bear his part. On the other hand, while so many men with desperate wounds recovered in due time, others were not so fortunate. The knee of one scout was slightly grazed. The wound was a mere scratch. He fought to the finish without any discomfort but died a week later of blood poisoning.

It may be accepted as a general truth that Indians do not like to fight in the open, usually preferring an ambuscade or an attack under cover even when the odds are largely in their favour. But on this occasion their leader, Roman Nose, was a chieftain quite out of the ordinary. He was of magnificent physique and was superbly mounted. Naked save for a breechcloth and a long war hood of eagles' plumes, he rode into battle with a dash and courage that promised to carry all before it. He marshalled his men for an irresistible charge, and rode down their line to hearten them for the attack, as gallant a figure as was Henry of Navarre before Ivry. Suddenly from his throat a war whoop was lifted to the skies; a moment later his braves reëchoed it, and then began the crisis of that memorable day, so full of critical moments.

Each scout lay low in his rifle pit, grimly resolved to die hard if die he must. A hail of bullets swept over them, but no single shot echoed back to the charging Cheynnes from the silent pits. On and on the natives dashed till at one sharp word of command the pits blazed with a flashing line of fire. It did not even give the Indians pause. A second volley poured on them from the repeaters—a third—a fourth. Great gaps opened in their lines. Horses and riders floundered in the sand, but still Roman Nose, a good ten yards in the lead, cheered them on. The pits again flamed out. The clearing smoke showed that their medicine man was down, but still the Cheyennes followed their gallant chief. A sixth volley brought down Roman Nose, almost at the island. The Indians saw it, wavered, and at the next volley broke to right and left as a wave does against a rock. But some of them, either being mad with the lust of fight or having lost control of their horses, were shot down even as they leaped their horses over the scanty entrenchments. So ended their last attempt to take the position by storm. After this it became a matter of starving the defenders.

It was about this time that Lieutenant Beecher was killed. He and Oakes lay side by side with their faces in opposite directions, each protected by a sandpit. In addition to the pit, a dead horse lay in front of Oakes, a dead mule before Beecher. An Indian sharpshooter fired across the neck of the horse and struck Beecher at the base of the backbone. This was about noon, and the young officer lived in great agony till dusk, when he died.

That night the command prepared for a siege. The intrenchments were deepened, Burke's well was improved, and from the dead horses steaks were cut for future needs. It was absolutely essential that the commandant at Fort Wallace, some hundred and ten miles distant, should be informed of the plight of the command, and to that end volunteers were called for to steal through the Indian lines and undertake the journey. Out of the score of volunteers, Pierre Trudeau and a young man named Jack Stillwell were selected to make the attempt. Next day the fight was renewed, but owing to their improved intrenchments less damage was done, though the wounded suffered greatly from the heat. Two more scouts were sent out the second night, but they were unable to pierce the enemy's lines and were forced to return. At nightfall of the third day Donovan and Pliley also were sent out to try the long journey to seek reënforcements, lest the first two scouts should fall into the hands of the enemy. Colonel Forsyth had been wounded again, and the condition of the wounded was far from being enviable, as there were no medical supplies on hand. Day after day dragged through. The food supply gave out, the horse steaks having gone bad from the heat. Colonel Forsyth proposed to the sound men that they move out at night and strike toward Fort Wallace, leaving the wounded to keep back the Indians, who by this time, on account of their very heavy losses, were plainly weary of their task. But next day—the ninth since the attack—the advance guard of the relieving column, under Lieutenant Colonel L. H. Carpenter, appeared in sight. The joy of the defenders may better be imagined than described. They had for more than a week held back a force nearly twenty times as large as their own. Half of their own force had been killed or wounded, and they had suffered much from lack of food and medicine. Surely no more plucky defence is registered in the annals of Indian warfare.

"BUCKY" O'NEILL

Arizona Sheriff—a Knight-Errant of the Nineteenth Century. A Poet, Adventurer, and Scholar—But Always Militant

Out of the old hard-riding, fighting, roistering Southwest have come many notable characters, but never another just like "Bucky" O'Neill. More than any other man I can think of at the moment he typifies the romance of the West. In Arizona hundreds of hearts still warm to the memory of the gallant devil-may-care Rough Rider who died in Cuba with a smile on his lips and his face to the foe.

These old-timers knew him as a fearless leader of men in a new wild country where only the strong could hold supremacy, but it is not chiefly as a fighting man that Bucky's name has come down to the present generation. The frontier breeds individualists. O'Neill was the most many-sided man Arizona has produced. He was a poet, an adventurer, and a scholar. He was editor, lawyer, judge, sheriff, politician, and soldier. He was the wildest of gamblers, the most daring of officers, the shyest of men. A knight-errant of the Nineteenth Century, he was always ready to couch a lance for the weak and the distressed. A child's appeal, a woman's tears, disarmed him at once. Yet when the occasion came he could be hard and cold as chilled steel.

It was this strange temperamental blend, this mixture of the adventurer and the son of civilization, that lent Bucky his peculiar charm. He was an educated gentleman, a student of the classics. But this same man, who quoted Whitman on the battlefield while the bullets spattered around him, earned his nickname of "Bucky" by his reckless plunging in the gambling houses of Arizona where Mexicans, Chinamen, Indians, tourists, cowpunchers, miners, cattlemen, and desperadoes rubbed shoulders at the faro table and the roulette wheel. The outstanding note of the man was his vitality, the unrestrained energy of his manhood. Whatever he did was done with his whole heart. He could do foolish, prodigal things, but he could not do a mean one.

Bucky carried in his appearance a letter of recommendation. A friendly smile from soft brown eyes greeted the stranger. He was lithe and sinewy as a tiger, with that easy graceful mastery of his power one never finds in loud-mouthed braggarts. One would never learn from the lips of this soft-voiced young man that he was one of the most dramatic dare-devils the West had produced. Like a flash of lightning when the call to action came, he had not a word to say for himself after the crisis had been met and was past.

I have listened to scores of stories illustrating the dash of Bucky, his shyness, his generosity, his love of fair play, his indignation at injustice. This last instinct in him often found expression.

When the Santa Fe Railway was building into Arizona a gang of graders jumped a spring that belonged to the Navajo Indians. The natives were a peaceful pastoral people. They complained without avail. Their herds of sheep began to die of thirst. They were in pitiable condition when a young man rode into their camp one day. He heard their story and his brown eyes flamed. He did not wait for legal relief or for a sheriff's posse. Swinging to the saddle, he rode to the graders' camp. To the foreman of the outfit he explained that the spring would have to be restored to its owners.

The big Irishman looked over this soft-spoken youth and grinned. "Better get home to your mother, me lad," he suggested.

Bucky did not raise his voice, but there was a curious metallic quality to it. "By God, you'll give 'em back their spring," he said.

"Make us, me buckaroo," retorted the foreman, amused.

The Irish blood of young O'Neill began to simmer. "Suits me if it does you," he replied, and he rode away.

A few hours later Bucky was again at the camp, this time with the armed Navajos at his back. The foreman was a rough fighting giant. He had to be to hold his job, for graders in those days were a hard lot. But Indians on the warpath were too much of an enterprise to tackle lone-handed. Very likely his bosses would not stand for it. He tried soft words.

"Now, me lad, you wouldn't be a renegade, would ye, an' throw in with them damned redskins against white men?" he wheedled.

Bucky had only one thing to say. He said it in three words: "Get out *pronto*."

The construction gang got out, *muy pronto*.

The chief of the Navajos was so grateful to Bucky that he presented him with his great silver ring, the highest mark of favour he could bestow. Later in life Bucky gave this ring to Thurlow Weed Barnes.

Bucky would give away anything he had to a friend or to one in need. A story is told of him that he went to a bank in Prescott and drew $300 to pay a debt at a store. Before he reached his creditor he was stopped twice to listen to hard-luck tales. The money he had drawn was transferred from his pocket to those of the down-and-outers. The store-keeper had to wait for his money.

Once more Bucky clashed with railroad interests, on this occasion with the men at the top. He was an ardent politician, for years identified with the Republican party. After locating in Yavapai County in 1883 he filled at one time or another most of the important offices there. When he ran for sheriff he had inserted in the party platform a plank to the effect that the Republican candidates, if elected, would assess the railroad the full value of its land holdings. Since these included every other section on both sides of the track throughout the whole length of Yavapai County, it will be seen that this was important.

At that time the railroad, very essential to the growth of the territory as a connecting link with the East, was the strongest political force in that part of the country. The sheriff was ex-officio assessor and tax collector. Therefore the railroad declared war on Bucky's candidacy.

The issue of the campaign was Bucky. In saloons and mines and on ranches men fought out the question he had raised. It is said the railroad rushed in section hands for hundreds of miles to vote against him. He ran far ahead of his ticket and was elected.

He fulfilled preëlection pledges so efficiently that when there was a train robbery at Cañon Diablo the railroad officials did not ask for help in capturing the outlaws from the new sheriff. The only information given him was that the amount secured from the express car was of no consequence.

But Bucky was sheriff. A robbery had been committed in his territory and he took the trail. The Cañon Diablo is in a rough country, one in which the trail would be difficult to follow. The sheriff secured the services of Tom Horn, one of the best trailers in the West, who served for years against the Apaches with Lawton, Chaffee, Crook, and Miles. Through barren mountain ranges, across country where honest men had seldom ridden, Bucky and his posse followed the outlaws. The pursuit lasted for weeks. Several times the officers engaged at close quarters the bandits, who turned on them near the Utah-Colorado line and attempted an ambush. Repeatedly the robbers had doubled on their trail, trying to shake off the relentless chase. The mounts of the sheriff's party were worn and jaded. The nearest ranch was thirty miles distant, and they were headed for it when there came a volley from behind a buttress of rock.

Bucky led the charge of his men. The outlaws jumped to their saddles and fled. In the running fight that followed one of the robbers was killed. The others escaped.

With fresh mounts Tom Horn took up the trail again. The delay, as well as the roughness of the country, favoured the bandit. But once more the posse caught up with their prey. Another of the fugitives was downed. Bucky clung close to the others.

He was riding an enduring buckskin horse named Sandy. Twice Sandy had swum the Colorado River with his master on his back. Bucky was ready to bet that Sandy could cover any specified stretch of country in shorter time than any horse in Arizona. The buckskin was hitting the trail with the same road gait as when he had started. Bucky's impatience got the better of his prudence. He rode far ahead of his party and came upon the outlaws camped in Wah Weep Cañon. They were taking their ease before the fire, under the impression that they had shaken off the sheriff.

An alien voice disturbed their calm. "'Lo, boys, what's new?" came O'Neill's easy greeting.

The train robbers stared open mouthed at him. His guns covered them.

"Stick 'em up, boys." Bucky pleasantly advised.

They continued to look at him. Their hands itched to reach the six-shooters that were so near and yet so far. Slowly and reluctantly their arms went up. It would not do to monkey with this fellow. They knew all about him. His reputation had travelled far.

He held them under his guns for an hour before Tom Horn brought in the rest of his party. A very large sum of money was secured, stolen from the express car. On the return trip Bucky picked up a shoe that Sandy had cast. For long this was a treasured relic in the O'Neill family.

This was probably the most expensive pleasure trip Bucky ever took. He met all the bills of the posse both ways and those of the prisoners on the return journey. The county board of supervisors, friends of the railroad, refused to reimburse Bucky because according to law he should have asked that body for permission to leave the county. The sheriff filed suit, fought it from court to court, and lost it in the one of last appeal.

A good sheriff in those days when the frontier was untamed had no primrose path to follow. On one occasion Bucky followed a man named Smith across the line into New Mexico. He caught up with the desperado, and they exchanged shots. Smith fell from his horse, leg shattered. Bucky administered first aid, helped him to his horse, and took him to the nearest village. Smith had friends here, and they gathered in force, demanding the release of the prisoner. It appears that Smith was a chivalrous bandit. He might have escaped if he had not found a young schoolteacher wandering on the desert and brought her back to town, thus delaying his departure. His friends intimated that under the circumstances it would not be fair to let him suffer on account of his kind heart.

The sheriff appreciated the point, but ruled that it was not applicable to the present occasion. He backed his prisoner into a *tendejón* and advised the crowd that the building was now fully occupied.

Smith shouted to the crowd over the sheriff's shoulder that Bucky had shot him over a woman and that this was a personal grudge. Those outside surged forward.

Bucky's answer was to the point, easily understood. He merely said that he would shoot the first man who reached the doorstep and then the prisoner. A parley followed. A wire was dispatched to Prescott, and the answer cleared up the situation. An hour later the sheriff departed accompanied by one hand-cuffed outlaw.

His love of fair play made Bucky an advocate of women's rights. He worked to secure them the ballot in Arizona, and though not a member of the legislature he was a first-class lobbyist when his sympathies were engaged. Largely through his influence a bill was passed giving women who owned property the right to vote at bond elections.

When Tombstone was a roaring camp Bucky O'Neill was editor of one of its papers for a short time. He worked to get what is now Cochise County cut off from Pima and made into a separate county. In recognition of his services the citizens presented him with a handsome watch. He lost this during a train robbery in Sonora. Not long afterward a stranger slouched into Joe Wilson's store at Prescott and left a small package for O'Neill. It contained his watch. Bucky was always of opinion that it had been returned to him by some man whom he had driven out of Arizona, one who was now operating as a hold-up in Mexico.

When there was danger Bucky's brain always functioned. The Hardy gang of outlaws rode in from the hills and camped on the edge of Phoenix. They sent in word that they were coming in to shoot up the town. Henry Garfio, a Mexican, was sheriff. He was a notably game and nervy man. Bucky offered to serve as deputy on this occasion.

A fusillade of shots reached their ears. They stepped out into the road. In a cloud of dust the cowboys came galloping down Washington Street. From rifles and revolvers they were flinging shots skyward.

O'Neill flung up a hand and ordered Hardy to stop. The horseman fired at him. Almost simultaneously Hardy tumbled from his horse, a wound in his leg.

Bucky stepped up to him. "Didn't I say you'd better stop?" he asked mildly, almost apologetically.

Though Bucky seems not to have known what fear

is in the ordinary sense of the word, his shyness more than once sent him into a panic. All his life he had to struggle against this. Early in life he used to practise his speeches in the woods, sure that he would have "buck fever" when the time came to deliver them.

Soon after he was elected judge a couple came to him to be married. The bride did not blush as much as Bucky, and her replies were not so faint as his questions. For Bucky had been joshed a great deal around the courthouse. His friends had told him he would have to kiss the bride, and this had much disturbed him. Probably he omitted some part of the ceremony, but he got the candidates safely married. The bride, however, seemed to feel that things were incomplete. She held a whispered colloquy with the groom and returned.

"Haven't you forgotten something, sir?" asked she coyly.

The judge picked the window from which he would jump.

"W-what?" he gasped.

"Why, the ring. Seems to me it would look a heap better on my finger than in your vest pocket."

Bucky came to life again and dug out the ring.

Once, at least, Bucky was decisively routed by a woman. This was in Yavapai County when he was judge. The public administrator had not made a report for several years of estates intrusted to him. Judge O'Neill called for such a report. The wife of the official, an Irish lady of prowess, appeared in court for him. There was ire in her eye and an umbrella in her hand.

Early in the proceedings she opened fire, with tongue and umbrella. Bucky hastily declared court adjourned as he went through the nearest window. Encouraged by her success, the lady camped on Bucky's trail and sued him at each succeeding term of court for several years.

A dozen stories could be told, each true, to illustrate Bucky's courage. There was the time when he was sheriff of Yavapai and some bad men came into town announcing that they did not intend to be arrested. They tied up at the hitch rack of Cavanaugh's saloon. Much drinking and boasting. Enter Bucky quietly. Exit the bad men to jail in charge of soft-spoken Bucky.

There was the time when Neal the stage driver (who still lives at Oracle, where I knew him thirty years ago) was taking Bucky to Mammoth for a political meeting. The river was swollen by recent floods. Neal, a game man who fought off bandits on one occasion when they stuck up his stage, looked at his passenger and murmured, "What now?"

"Mammoth is where I'm headed for," O'Neill suggested.

Neal looked at the raging waters and figured that it would be a near thing but that his broncs could just about make it.

"It's yore say-so," Neal replied indifferently—indifferently from surface indications at least.

"All right, shoot. I say Mammoth."

They were nearly drowned, but Bucky spoke at Mammoth that night.

To take still another case, there was the time when Bucky was walking along Congress Street, in Tucson, with a rough-spoken citizen who prided himself on plain talk. As they passed the Legal Tender, a famous saloon and gambling house, O'Neill made what he thought was an innocuous remark. The other man told him that he lied.

"What's that?" asked Bucky.

"I say you lie," was the swift, brusque retort.

Instantly Tucson was treated to the spectacle of a fake bad man being churned up and down by his ears.

Bucky would tackle anything. He was for the under dog, and when the call came his hat was always in the ring. In a speech at the Grand Cañon Roosevelt mentioned that it was an inspiration to fight beside Bucky O'Neill. So other men felt. That is why you may to-day see on the square at Prescott a replica of Bucky in the bronze statue of a horse and rider commemorative of the Rough Riders who went to Cuba from Arizona.

It is said that Bucky was the first volunteer mustered into service for the war with Spain. This may or may not be true. He was sworn in as a private on the twenty-ninth day of April. Later he was given a commission in the Arizona troop of the Rough Riders. Intensely patriotic, it was the hope of Bucky that Arizona would win statehood if her sons proved worthy on the field of battle.

"Who wouldn't gamble for a star?" he said as he signed up to fight.

That remark has been variously interpreted. Some think he meant the star which represents the military rank of a brigadier general, but his friends say he meant another star in the flag of his country.

Nobody could lose a bet with more equanimity than Bucky. He always played for high stakes. Even if he had known he was going to lose his life, he would not have hesitated.

At the time he was killed Bucky's men were lying in a trench. He stood up talking with Captain House of the artillery. He had been quoting Whitman's "Captain, My Captain." One of his men begged him to take cover. "The Spanish bullet hasn't yet been moulded that can kill me," he answered gaily. Next moment he fell, mortally wounded.

Bucky's nerve was of so peculiar a quality that he once failed in his duty as a soldier. The Prescott Grays, a company of militia in which he was second lieutenant, were called out as guards at a public hanging. The troops surrounded the scaffold. As the trap was sprung an officer keeled over in a faint. It was Bucky O'Neill. He could not bear to see a man killed without having a chance to fight for his life.

William (Bucky) O'Neill was born in St. Louis of first-class stock. His parents were John Owen O'Neill and Mary O'Neill. When the Civil War broke out John Owen O'Neill raised a company of volunteers. He served throughout the four years as captain of Company K, One Hundred and Sixteenth Pennsylvania Volunteers, a part of the celebrated Irish brigade so often mentioned in the annals of the war. He distinguished himself in the battle of Fredericksburg, being wounded five times. During the war he received fourteen wounds and was obliged to walk on crutches for the rest of his life. The last years of his life were spent as provost marshal of the District of Columbia.

A *Who's Who* of Bucky would convey the information that he was one of four children, that he was graduated in the liberal arts department of Gonzales College and later in the law department of the National University with the class of '79. He went West, young man, specifically to Phoenix, Arizona, where he went into newspaper work as editor and manager of the *Herald*. He drifted to the Tombstone mining field, still as a reporter and editor. Next he practised law in the southern part of the territory and eked out a living as court stenographer. In 1883 he located in Prescott. He was editor of *Hoof and Horn*, a journal devoted to the interests of stockmen, and was president of the Buckeye Canal Company. He owned land and had varied business activities. But all the time he was a politician of the better sort, devoted to the public service, a broad-minded American who had far more than a local outlook.

Yet he was first and last a Westerner. From the day of his arrival he flung himself with abandon into the life of Arizona. He loved it, its freedom, its recklessness, its individual flavour. When the news reached the sunburned territory that its favourite son had passed out with a Spanish bullet in his throat the hearts of men and women grew heavy with the sense of personal loss, much as many of us felt when we read that his chief, Theodore Roosevelt, had left us forever. In life they did not all approve him, but they knew a very brave and gallant soul had turned the last corner with a smile and a wave of the hand.

WHEN THE OUTLAW RODE
IN OKLAHOMA

"Uncle" Billy Tilghman, the Last of the Old-time Sheriffs. He Died with His Boots on.

AT CROMWELL, Oklahoma, there died recently almost the last of the great sheriffs who carried law and order to our Western border. From some points of view William Tilghman was the greatest peace officer the West ever had. Other marshals and sheriffs held office for two or three years and made reputations. Tilghman fought against crime for more than fifty years, was always in the harness, took a thousand chances, and survived till he was well into the seventies. He made more arrests of dangerous bad men, broke up more gangs of outlaws, sent more criminals to the penitentiary, than any individual officer on the frontier. And with it all he was quiet, gentlemanly, soft-spoken, never overbearing, a friend of all the little boys in the neighbourhood.

"Uncle" Billy fell in the line of duty, shot to death by a drunken federal prohibition officer whom he was arresting for making a disturbance in front of a dance hall. It was characteristic of Tilghman that, though he "died with his boots on," in the old cow-town phraseology, he had not drawn his revolver from its scabbard. That was his way. He always gave the other fellow the benefit of the doubt. Other noted gunmen shot first and asked questions afterward. Not Tilghman. He took his fighting chance every time. The wise ones shook their heads and said that some day some drunken tough would get Bill, but Tilghman paid no attention to their prophecies. It was his business to take chances, so he took them.

For instance, there was the capture of Bill Doolin, leader of the gang of train robbers of that name, one of the fiercest, gamest men on the frontier.

The Doolin gang was terrorizing Oklahoma, as the James-Younger gang had done in Missouri years before, and as the Daltons had done in and around the country formerly known as the Indian Territory. It held up banks and trains and raided towns. When mothers wanted to quiet their children they warned that Bill Doolin would get them if they were not good. The outlaw was on the way to become a legend, as Jesse James and Billy the Kid had been before him.

But Billy Tilghman and other fearless officers nipped the legend business in the bud.

It was not easy to capture the Doolins because they had so many friends among the ranchmen, just as Jesse James had among the Missouri farmers of his day. Tilghman thought it would be a good idea to arrest some of the ranchers who were known to harbour bandits and were suspected of cattle stealing.

Taking Neal Brown with him as deputy, Tilghman left Guthrie with two saddle horses tied behind a covered wagon. They had food and a camping outfit.

It was a bitter cold day in January, 1895, when the officers reached the ranch at Rock Fort, where the principal suspects lived. Snow blanketed the ground, and the sodden sky promised more. Smoke curled from the chimney of the cabin, though no horses or men were to be seen outside. Tilghman's way was always the simple bold way. He left his rifle in the wagon, walked through the snow to the house, knocked on the door, and when no answer came pushed it open and went inside.

A fire of blackjack logs roared cheerfully up the chimney, in front of which sat the man for whom he was looking, a rifle across his knees. The rancher looked at the officer surlily without speaking.

As Tilghman moved forward to the fire he observed that on each side of the room there was a tier of bunks hung with curtains so that he could not tell whether the beds were occupied or not. His hands were half frozen from the cold. Moreover, he had some questions to ask. He turned his back to the fire and put his hands behind him.

Instantly the muscles in Tilghman's body grew rigid and his brain began to work lightning fast. From each bunk, at the edge of the curtain, the barrel of a rifle projected an inch or more. He had walked into a trap. Eight desperate men, dead shots, had him covered and any moment might blaze away at him. If they thought he had a posse with him they would not hesitate for an instant.

Tilghman's nerve stood the test. Not by the twitch

of an eyelid or the slightest quaver of the voice did he betray the fact that he knew he was in deadly peril. He talked quietly, casually, about the happenings in Cattleland, touched on the gossip of the day, and inquired about the best road to reach a destination he invented on the spur of the moment. He even joked about arranging a fight between his dog and one of Doolin's. Then, without haste, as though reluctant to leave the good fire, he said he reckoned he must be going.

At an even pace he moved to the door, nodded a careless "So long," and stepped outside.

To Neal Brown he gave quiet orders: "Drive on, not too fast, and don't look round."

In that room were Bill Doolin, Little Dick, Tulsa Jack, Charley Pierce, and others. No man ever had a closer shave. Only the most consummate display of cool nerve saved Tilghman and his deputy. As it was, he had no sooner closed the door than one of the bandits, known as Red Buck, jumped from a bunk and swore to kill him at once. Bill Doolin saved the marshal's life. He closed with Red Buck, struggling with the furious man.

"Bill Tilghman is too good a man to shoot in the back," he said.

Doolin married a preacher's daughter, Edith Ellsworth. They loved each other devotedly, and more than once Doolin made up his mind to reform. Once he even left the country, but could not live up to his good resolutions. Still he led his band on wild raids. He contracted rheumatism and went to Eureka

Springs, Arkansas, to take the baths. Through an intercepted letter Tilghman learned he was there.

That night Tilghman entrained for Eureka Springs. Not to be recognized instantly and so be forced to shoot at sight, he wore a long coat and a silk hat.

After careful inquiry Tilghman learned that Doolin was at a bathhouse. The officer walked into the parlour of the place and saw Doolin seated in a corner where he could observe anyone who entered. The unusual clothes deceived him for a moment, and Tilghman covered him with his revolver.

"Hands up, Bill!" he ordered.

The tall, lank, sandy-haired desperado looked at him. Doolin had sworn never to be taken alive, and Tilghman knew it.

The bandit jumped up, reaching for the weapon hanging under his left arm. Tilghman did not fire, for word had come to him of how Doolin had saved his life a year before. He caught at the outlaw's arm and with his shoulder drove him back to the wall, his own revolver pressed against the stomach of the bad man.

"Don't make me kill you, Bill!" he urged.

The weight of Tilghman's body pinned the bank robber to the wall and prevented his hand from reaching the revolver under his coat. Doolin struggled to escape from the disadvantage of position. He tried desperately to get at his gun.

With every ounce of strength he had, Tilghman held him fast. The barrel of the officer's revolver gouged into the other man's stomach. At any moment it might go off. Still Doolin fought. As they struggled Tilghman begged him to surrender and not force him to shoot. Doolin gave up at last.

"Yore six-full takes the pot," he admitted.

Tilghman took the outlaw to Guthrie, where Doolin engineered a wholesale prison escape. Later he was killed in a duel with Marshal Heck Thomas. Heck Thomas was one of the "three guardsmen." The other two were Bill Tilghman and Chris Madsen. These three officers were so called because of their relentless pursuit of criminals. Sometimes they worked together, sometimes separately. Thomas was a Georgian by birth and as a boy of twelve served with Stonewall Jackson in the Confederate army. Later he was appointed a deputy United States marshal and worked out of Fort Smith, where the celebrated Judge Parker passed the death sentence on so many men that on various occasions four, five, and six men were hanged at the same time. Tilghman and Thomas took forty-one prisoners to this court on one train, nine of whom were given a death sentence by Judge Parker. The daring exploits of Thomas would fill a book. He helped break up the Dalton and the Doolin gangs. In his duel with Bill Doolin the outlaw had the first two shots. Heck Thomas fired once with his shotgun. Once was enough.

Chris Madsen was an old soldier and Indian fighter. He was later a deputy United States marshal in Texas, Oklahoma, and the Indian Territory. He captured bad men too numerous to mention. It was his posse that killed Tulsa Jack after the Dover train robbery, and it was he personally who arrested the three men who robbed a train at Logan, New Mexico.

Oklahoma and the Indian Territory were filled with wild men who refused to subdue themselves to the needs of civilization when the country settled up. They had lived an untrammelled life in the open. It is significant that every outlaw in the country had been at one time a cowboy. They were dare-devils who had little respect for law in the abstract, though most of them lived up to their own rough code. In the end law was too strong for them, chiefly because of such men as the three guardsmen. It is noteworthy that scarcely a single member of the Dalton or the Doolin gangs, with the exception of Emmett Dalton, who is still living, escaped a violent death.

The Daltons came of respectable people. There was a large family of them, some of whom remained peaceable ranchers. But the love of adventure was in the blood. Several of them became law officers. Frank, Grattan, and Bob Dalton were at one time deputy United States marshals, and Frank was killed in the line of duty in a gun fight. They were fearless men all, hard riders, dead shots, rough livers. The step across the border into outlawry was not a hard one for them to take. They began to rob trains and banks. Their brothers Emmett and Bill Dalton joined them. So did Bill Doolin, Charley Bryant, Ol Yountis, Dick Broadwell, and Bill Powers. At their holdups sometimes one and sometimes another of the gang was present. Young Bob Dalton, twenty-two years old, was their leader. They got their hand in by robbing a train in California. In 1891 they held up a train at Red Rock, Oklahoma. They robbed another at Perry, in the Cherokee Strip, and a fourth at Adair.

The hunters got busy. Charley Bryant was wounded and captured. Ed Short arrested him. Bryant secured a gun, and the two men killed each other while the officer was taking the bandit to prison. Yountis was shot down by a posse which included Chris Madsen and Heck Thomas. But the Daltons themselves were still at large.

Trying to outdo the James brothers, Bob Dalton decided to rob two banks at once and selected Coffeyville, Kansas, as the scene of operations. It was bad medicine for them. The story of that raid parallels very closely that of the Northfield, Minnesota, one staged by the James and Younger gang. Both of them showed the boldness, the courage, the recklessness of these border ruffians, and both showed, too, a certain fine loyalty characteristic of some of these men. The Youngers stayed by each other to the death, remaining with a wounded brother against the advice of Jesse James, who proposed to kill in cold blood the disabled man to facilitate their own escape. So did the Daltons stand by one another.

These raids, too, showed the readiness of the plain American to rise swiftly to an emergency. In ten minutes of desperate fighting, both at Northfield and at Coffeyville, the bank robbers were almost wiped out.

Two of the Dalton gang might have escaped after the failure of the enterprise, but they went back to try to help their fellows. Later, after four citizens had been killed and four of the bandits were either dead or dying, Emmett Dalton, a boy of twenty, already wounded, turned his horse and rode through a line of fire to attempt a rescue of his brother Grat. In doing so he was almost fatally wounded and was captured.

The Doolin gang began to ride on its raids shortly after this, probably encouraged to crime by the deeds of the Daltons. It was easy to get recruits. Bill Dalton, Red Buck, Bitter Creek, Little Dick and Little Bill, and Arkansas Tom joined Doolin. They robbed many trains and banks, taking horses whenever they needed them to facilitate escape. At Cimarron, Kansas, in the month of May, 1893, the Doolin gang robbed a train and had a hard time to get back to safety. It was cornered at Ingalls and attacked by a posse of officers. In the pitched battle which followed Doolin killed Marshal Speed, and Bill Dalton, while rescuing Bitter Creek, who had fallen wounded from his horse, killed Lafe Shadley.

The Doolins robbed a bank at Southwest City, Missouri, and had to fight their way out of town. During this battle a prominent citizen of the town, formerly state auditor, was killed by Little Bill while the outlaws were making for their horses to escape. By way of the Creek and the Cherokee Nations the bandits reached Oklahoma. Not long after this a trap was laid for them at Canadian City, but the gang escaped, leaving Sheriff McGee dead.

After this the country grew hot for the outlaws.

The three guardsmen were assigned the job of capturing them. The task was very difficult because none of the officers could make a move without friends of the outlaws carrying word to them of what was being done.

It was now that Billy Tilghman had his adventure at Rock Fort ranch, and it was shortly afterward that he captured Bill Doolin at Eureka Springs.

The toils were closing in on the outlaws. Tulsa Jack was killed by a posse headed by Chris Madsen. Bill Dalton's hiding place was discovered, and he was killed while trying to escape. Pierce and Bitter Creek fell into an ambush arranged by Tilghman and Thomas and were slain by two farmers. Little Bill was badly wounded and captured by Tilghman in a duel fought at the Sam Moore ranch. Doolin, as has been told, was captured by Tilghman and killed by Heck Thomas. The other members of the gang scattered, only to renew their lawlessness and to fall victims later to the march of a civilization which wiped them out.

Not long afterward Tilghman met Bill Raidler, another member of the Doolin gang, on a road in the Osage Indian country. He had been looking for Raidler a long time, for the outlaw was wanted for several bank and train robberies. Raidler, a desperate character, had sent word to Tilghman to come and get him if he wanted him. So the marshal had come.

He ordered the bandit to throw up his hands. Raidler in answer fired. Tilghman poured a charge of buckshot into the outlaw that killed him before he was out of the saddle.

Bat Masterson, himself one of the most famous sheriffs of the West, leaves it on record that it would take a volume the size of an encyclopædia to record the exploits of Billy Tilghman. The odd thing is that, though fired at a hundred times, he was for many years never touched by a bullet.

Billy Tilghman had been a buffalo hunter on the banks of the Medicine Lodge River in the early days. He was a boy of seventeen when he went out, among the first of the white men adventuring to "take the hides off'n them," as the buffalo hunters put it. General Custer had put down an Indian uprising in this part of the country only the year before, and the tribes were sulky and unfriendly. They had been located on reservations, but frequently broke bounds to raid, murder, and pillage.

The Tilghman party came back to camp one evening, after a day of hunting, to find their hides destroyed, their provisions stolen, and their camp burned. The situation was precarious. The natives might be lurking in the vicinity to kill them. It was very likely they would return. After a discussion of ways and means the other hunters proposed to move to Mule Creek, twenty miles farther from the reservation.

This did not suit the slim boy who was even then the real leader of the party. He was not ready to move and leave the green hides not found by the Indians.

"We'll peg out the hides to dry. If Mr. Indian comes back I expect I'll be here," he said.

His partners assented. Next day Tilghman did not hunt with them. He hid near the camp in a position that commanded the approach to it.

The Indians must have seen the hunters leave, for presently seven of them appeared on horseback, dismounted, and approached. During the night one of the partners had travelled thirty miles and brought back fresh provisions. One of the Indians picked up a sack of flour and threw it across the back of his pony. A battle ensued, during which Tilghman killed four out of the seven.

This established his reputation for fearlessness. During the spring of 1874 there was an uprising of Cheyennes, Arapahoes, Comanches, and Kiowas. This was formidable and lasted for nearly a year. Tilghman was a government scout and had many close shaves while carrying dispatches. Later he served through the campaign of 1878, when Dull Knife set out from Fort Sill on the warpath with his band of plundering and murdering redskins. Tilghman distinguished himself by riding seventy-five miles through the Indian country to carry word to the soldiers of the dangers of a beleaguered party. Guided by Billy, the cavalry arrived in time to save some of the defenders, though the blockhouse was already in flames.

Tilghman moved to a ranch near Dodge City, then the wildest town in the United States. This was in the days of the great cattle drives, some years nearly half a million head passing the town. The Texans driving these were wild, untamed youths, and they had money to spend. Gamblers and bad men flocked to the town to share the harvest. They were a lawless crew. Each man carried his own protection in the holster strapped to his side. Those who engaged in fight and were not quick on the trigger took up permanent residence in Boot Hill, as the graveyard was named because so many of those buried there died with their boots on.

To preserve law and order it was necessary to have officials of courage. The famous Bat Masterson and his brother Ed were marshals during part of the stormy days. Tilghman, with Ben Daniels as assistant, was marshal during the year of the fire. Robert M. Wright, mayor of Dodge City that year, writes that no braver man ever handled a gun or arrested an outlaw. The marshal passed through many narrow escapes, for it seemed that "every bad and desperate character in the whole West gathered here, and when we would drive out one lot another set would put in an appearance." Ben Daniels was later appointed United States marshal by President Roosevelt, who said Ben was one of the bravest men he had ever known.

During the three years of his incumbency Tilghman cleared up Dodge so efficiently that the bad men departed for other climes. There was no profit in operating where a man as fearless as the marshal, and one so dead a shot, represented the law. He took his job too seriously to suit them. Therefore they emigrated.

It was Tilghman's rule never to take a life unless he was forced to do so to save his own. No matter how desperate a criminal might be, or how bad his reputation as a killer might be, Uncle Billy never shot until the other started hostilities. This vastly increased the risk of his business, since he always gave his opponent first chance and the tenth part of a second might mean the difference between life and death.

Such a man was always in demand to protect society. After he moved from Kansas to Oklahoma nearly all the governors of that state and several Presidents requisitioned his services. He was sent on the most desperate missions and always brought back his man.

The noted gunmen of the West were of three classes. The first of these was composed of those who were against law and society. They fought, like cornered wolves, without respect for the rights of others. They had gone bad, and, though they may at times have had generous impulses, the trend of their lives was toward evil. Apparently they enjoyed taking human life. The slightest opposition would set their guns to smoking. Billy the Kid was such a man. Bob Ollinger was another. A third was Doc Holliday. John Wesley Hardin was a fourth. A dozen of them swaggered up and down the streets of Virginia City and Carson before the Vigilantes became active.

The second class was of a more civilized type. It

did not set its face against stabilized order in general, though it reserved the right to carry on private vendettas and on occasion to step outside the law. Generally the men of this class were quiet, soft-spoken, and very efficient at the business of killing. Most of them were at one time or another peace officers in wild frontier towns. They were chosen because they were dead shots, had nerve, and had won reputations as gunmen that tended to curb both the criminals and the reckless miners or cowboys frequenting the town. Most of these—at least the ones that I have met—had cold light-blue eyes. They did not take chances with law breakers but shot swiftly, on sometimes inadequate provocations. Wild Bill, Luke Short, Bat Masterson, were of this type.

The third class of gunman was entirely a good citizen. He served society, never attempted to run towns, or to settle private scores by the use of official position. Billy Tilghman was one of these. For fifty years, first in Dodge City, Kansas, and later in Oklahoma, he fought against the lawless element relentlessly. During that time he captured scores of murderers, horse thieves, train robbers, bank holdups, and bad men. He killed in the interests of society, when he was forced to do so. But never once did he take the breaks or shoot without giving the other man a chance. In fact, he was blamed for going to the other extreme. In order to capture his man alive he would take long chances. It was always held to be a miracle that Uncle Billy had not been killed by some of the desperadoes whom he approached with his quiet formula, "You'd better give me your gun."

In the end he fell victim to his principle of choosing rather to take chances than to resort at once to the six-shooter. He stepped out of Ma Murphy's dance hall and grappled with a man disturbing the peace by wild shooting. He took the man's revolver from him without drawing his own. The other dragged out a second gun and poured bullets into Tilghman. The officer died within a few minutes.

Oklahoma knew that a good man had gone to his rest. His body lay in state in the capitol building, and men high in the affairs of the commonwealth—a United States senator, the governor, ex-governors, and many others—did honour to the quiet man who as town marshal, United States marshal, three times sheriff of Lincoln County, and state senator had served his country well.

Yes, Billy Tilghman was a good man. The boys of Cromwell will tell you so. They went to him for advice, and they followed it. They liked to talk with him, and if Uncle Billy said a thing was so—why, of course, it was so. That ended the matter.

THE WAR FOR THE RANGE

*The Sheep and Cattle Wars Led to Some of the
Bloodiest Conflicts of the West. Here Is the
Story of One of the Worst of Them*

RIDING one day under the untempered sun of the
desert in our arid West, the writer came on a little
pile of heaped-up boulders. The cowpuncher beside
him jerked a thumb toward it and explained grimly:
"Where 'Chapo' sleeps." Then, in three sentences,
out came the story. The little Mexican had paid for-
feit with his life for a scrupulous loyalty to his
employer's interest. He had died with his boots on
to the sound of snapping revolver and cracking Winchester. Near him lie scattered the bleaching bones
of a dozen cattle, and in the next arroyo are huddled
what remains of a flock of sheep. Together these
three exhibits offer a mute testimony to the fact that
sheep and cattle cannot exist on the open range side
by side.

In pioneer days the interests of sheepmen and
cattlemen did not conflict. Settlers were few, and
the range was large enough for both. But as the
country settled this was no longer true. Throughout
a large part of the West the cattle business, so far

as it depended upon the open range, became a ruined industry, and even in many more fortunate localities the cowmen had to fight desperately for a business existence. To understand how this came about it is necessary to appreciate the changed conditions that obtain now from those of fifty years ago. Then the star of the cattleman was in the ascendant. He was in the heyday of his glory. His cattle roamed over vast plains and fattened on the succulent grass at small expense to him. His reckless cowpunchers drove vast herds to market annually and made such towns as Abilene and Dodge City possible. The cowman and his vaqueros rode herd, kings of the range beyond dispute.

But all this changed. One source of immense trouble to the cattleman was the calf thief. Many a large outfit went out of business on account of the rustler. Where cow herders had to ride the range for fifty or seventy-five miles they were likely to be forestalled in branding a calf by some vigilant rustler whose little mountain ranch was near the usual grazing place of a bunch of cattle. Or very possibly the puncher for the big 3C ranch had caught and branded the calf with its proper mark; and when many months later he came upon a yearling branded BOB he had no means of knowing that the owner of the latter brand had deftly touched up the 3C with a running iron by the artistic addition of two strokes and an added letter. It may be stated parenthetically in passing that more than one large outfit got its start wholly from the free use of a running iron. In the more arid Southwest rustling was not so common because water is often pumped and cattle were in the habit of coming home and could be watched more closely, but even there it was a factor of no slight importance.

The small rancher pushed his way into the remotest section of the country and took up here and there the irrigable land for farming purposes. His fences rose to block the open range. Year by year the unfenced domain grew more restricted till there remained only the government reserves and such lands as were too arid or too rough for cultivation. The grazing lands, still immense according to Eastern standards, became constricted. The range was already overstocked with cattle to the detriment of the grass and the filaree, and years of protracted drought throughout the Southwest added to the hardships of the cattlemen. Then grew imminent a danger to the cattle industry more portentous of disaster than rustling, disease, overstocking, or drought. Mary's little lamb had come bleating across the desert.

Forty years ago mutton was not eaten in this country to any extent. There was no demand for sheep except for their wool, and owing to tariff conditions Argentine wool, which is of the same grade as the Montana product, had a market value of only five or six cents a pound. Sheep were to be bought at eighty-seven cents a head. But the conditions which regulated the production by controlling the market value began to change. The value of mutton as an article of food became recognized, and the owners commenced to breed up their stock. A new tariff schedule restored the import duty on wool, and at once the price of that staple rose. Montana wool was quoted at seventeen cents for the best grade, and the value of a good sheep was about three and a half dollars. Under the new conditions there was money in sheep, and the response to the stimulus was a great increase in production. Capital invested could be turned over fast, for an old ewe's wool would pay for her keep while there was a clear profit of nearly fifty per cent. in the yearly lamb.

All over the West the range began to be dotted with sheep ranches. The growth of the industry was nothing less than wonderful. The sheep grazed across the Dakotas, and worked their way over the mountains to Colorado, Wyoming, Montana, New Mexico, Arizona, and the Pacific States. No heights were inaccessible to them as grazing pastures, no valley too remote; and always they increased prodigiously. The census of the National Live Stock Association for the year 1900 showed the number of sheep in the country to be nearly 62,000,-000, more than half of which were in the Western division of states.

It followed inevitably that the forward lapping tide of settlement pushed the sheep and cattle together. Now it is a curious fact that the very odour of sheep drives cattle from a good range to a poorer one, even though the sheep may still be miles away. The difficulty might perhaps have been adjusted but for the fact that between cattle and sheep no lasting peace was possible. The fundamental trouble was that sheep are destructive to the range. They eat a country bare, and in a bad season will even crop down a forest of young pines. It is a common saying that sheep kill more than they eat. The well-known explorer, John Muir, hit on an apt phrase when he dubbed them "hoofed locusts." They feed in compact masses and their sharp chisel feet, driven by a hundredweight of solid flesh and bone, cut out every blade of grass, roots and all. The vegetation is killed for years to come, the ground often being stamped into a rocklike cement. Now in the arid lands every bit of vegetation, whether it be trunk, leaf, bough, or root serves as a conductor of water through the hard surface. Fallen leaves and twigs, no less than growing things, are a mulch. The conservation of the water supply depends on vegetation, just as vegetation in turn depends on it. If sheep would scatter in feeding, if they would simply eat the year's growth of vegetation, the damage would be much less. But a flock of them in passing kill the native grasses. Falling water finds no vegetation to absorb and hold it; necessarily it runs from the impervious ground without seeping in. In a country where the value of land may be stated in terms of water this was nothing less than a calamity, for the fine grazing grounds on which cattle had been wont to fatten were utterly ruined. Washes and ravines now ran where used to be a level country, these being due to the rainfall running off instead of being absorbed. Long years of drought in the Southwest added to the hardships of cattle, and in New Mexico, Arizona, and California the bleaching bones of hundreds of thousands of them dotted the deserts on account of lack of water.

It inevitably followed on the encroachments of the sheep that the cattlemen prepared to defend what they believed to be their rights. They held the ranges by priority of occupation, even though they could show no legal claim to them. From their point of view the advent of the sheepmen was a distinct interference with existing vested rights. Since they could not appeal to the law to protect them the riders of the plains became a law to themselves. They drew "dead lines" beyond which the sheepmen were not to bring their flocks. The sheepmen refused to recognize the existence of these dead lines and moved their flocks across them into the territory claimed by the stockmen. It was not to be expected that the reckless cowpunchers would tolerate submissively this defiance of their orders, for they understood that if the sheep were to remain their occupation would soon be gone. In many cases they fell on the flocks and drove them out of the country. The herders returned with reën-forcements and met force with force. Then followed raid and counter raid. Here and there over the grazing lands of the West—in Colorado, New Mexico, Texas, Arizona, Nevada, Idaho, Wyoming, and Montana—fierce and bloody conflicts were waged. The result was a strange one. Defeated in nine battles out of ten the sheepmen usually came out victor in the end. Everywhere, by reason of the law of the survival of the fittest, they encroached upon the grazing lands of their foes. Along the line of the Santa Fe, for instance, from Ash Fork to Seligman the sheepmen came to control most of the territory. They had the advantage of being able to carry their flocks for long periods without water when the grass was green; or they could tank water hauled in by the railroad, a plan not feasible for the watering of cattle on account of the quantity needed.

The sheepmen have usually been defeated in the individual battles because they are fewer in numbers than their opponents. A couple of herders with dogs can care for thousands of sheep, and the well-armed, swift-riding cowpunchers, swooping suddenly down on them, took them at such disadvantage that often they were obliged to stand aside helplessly and watch the slaughter of their charges. A former superintendent of the Hashknife outfit, so-called from the shape of the company's brand, detailed to the writer how his punchers had on one occasion raided a sheep camp and forced the herders to break camp at the point of their Winchesters. The herders had been cooking breakfast at the moment of the raid, and the playful vaqueros shouted with glee at their futile attempts to pack a red-hot sheet-iron stove on the back of an unwilling bronco.

A thousand stories could be told of the conflict between sheepmen and cattlemen. The owners of some large flocks amounting to about one hundred thousand head moved their entire herd across the dead line drawn by cattlemen of western Wyoming. At once the cowmen attacked them, disarmed the herders, destroyed wagons and sheep to the value of twenty thousand dollars, and warned the sheepmen to leave the country immediately on penalty of death. That night all was peace in the shadow of the Tetons, for cattle held the range alone while thousands of jaded sheep were plodding back to safety across the dead line. A few weeks after this occurrence nearly twelve thousand sheep were slaughtered near North Rock Springs in Wyoming. Many of these were shot and clubbed to death and the rest were driven over a precipice. The associated press dispatches announced briefly from time to time fatalities among herds of sheep caused by their eating blue vitriol which had been scattered over their grazing ground. One Sheridan owner had his flock destroyed by dynamite thrown among the animals while they were feeding. Owners at Laramie and Cheyenne have been annoyed greatly by sudden attacks from cowboys, who drove the flocks into foothills to be destroyed by coyotes and mountain lions. "Griff" Edwards was one of several sheep owners who fought back, but his enemies captured him, tied him to a tree, and killed his flocks before his eyes. In one season he is said to have lost more than fourteen thousand sheep. The sheepmen retaliated in kind. A cattle herder riding the range would see through his field glasses a motionless mass in the distance, and riding up to investigate would find a fine cow of his brand with a bullet through its forehead. Or perhaps a vaquero would disappear mysteriously, and months later a comrade would find his canteen beside the sun-bleached skeleton. So the silent, relentless war was carried on to the death.

The life of the cowpuncher was a much more varied and dramatic one than that of the sheepherder. Activity and rapid motion and the turmoil of the round-up made of him a product something akin to an overgrown boy still full of schoolday pranks. He could be classified among the gregarious animals. His general impression was that no man engaged in "walking sheep" could be a reputable citizen, but must of necessity be a low-down miserable creature whose rights need not be respected. To him the solitary life of the sheepherder carried with it a punishment beyond endurance. "I tended sheep once three months," a cowpuncher told the writer plaintively, "and I'd not do it again for a thousand dollars an hour." Indeed, few sights are more sombre and impressive than the solitary figure of a herder outlined against the sky, thousands of sheep about him and no human being or habitation in sight. For weeks he does not see his kind, and then only for a few minutes perhaps when a teamster brings a load of chuck to keep him for another month. He grows morbid and melancholy, and the desert comes to hold for him a horror not far distant from madness. Possibly this moroseness induced by their surroundings may be in a measure responsible for the sheepmen's readiness to engage in such a bloodthirsty war as the Graham-Tewksbury feud—a typical instance of the trouble engendered between these adverse interests—in which twenty-six cattlemen and six sheepmen lost their lives.

There are men now living who took part in this feud and others who pulled up stakes and left the Tonto Basin because of the desperate nature of this war. They found it impossible to remain neutrals and preferred to leave the country rather than be drawn in. In his remarkable book, *Scouting on Two Continents*, Major Burnham, undoubtedly the greatest scout since the days of Kit Carson, discusses this feud guardedly. He was no partisan, but in spite of himself he became a marked man, and his life was for months in danger. The story of his escape reads like a romance.

The Graham-Tewksbury affair—the most noted feud in the history of Arizona—is generally known as the Tonto Basin war. On one side were arrayed the Grahams assisted by cowpunchers connected with the Hashknife cattle outfit, on the other the Tewksburys and the sheep interest. The Tewksburys were of mixed blood, being part Indian and part Irish. Various reasons are given as the immediate cause for the origin of the feud. Originally the Grahams and Tewksburys were friends. It is claimed by some that Stinson, in whose interest the Grahams worked, tried to buy out the Tewksburys, and failing in that he swore to drive the "black Indians" out of the country. Others say that the attentions of one of the Grahams to the wife of one of the Tewksburys caused bad feeling. In any event, the trouble flared to a blaze when the Tewksburys brought sheep into Pleasant Valley early in '87. In grazing, some of these sheep encroached on land claimed by the Hashknife people as their range. The cattle began to desert their accus-

tomed watering places, and the herder was notified
at once to withdraw. He refused, and to intimidate
him the cowboys killed his dog, a valuable Scotch
collie, telling him that this was merely a warning.
The herder apprised the Tewksburys of the fact, who
immediately took steps to defend their interests.

Two men were sent to join the herder, who was
camped among the rocks in a ravine with large
boulders surrounding the camp so that a shot could
reach them only from one or two directions. The
cattlemen sought higher elevations in order to command the place and dropped occasional shots into the
hollow. The herders, cooped up in this temporary
fortress, were unable to attend their flocks which
were scattered in all directions by the cowboys. They
stole away in the night to the headquarters of the
Tewksburys. For several days after this there was
some sniping and pot-shotting, and though nobody
had as yet been injured it was understood by both
sides that the struggle was to be waged to the death.
The Tewksburys were largely outnumbered at this
time, but that was more than counterbalanced by
the fact that they were better skilled at bushwhacking
and trailing.

Several Texas cattlemen bought ranches in Pleasant Valley, and though they sided with the Grahams
to a certain extent, being mixed up with them in
rustling cattle as the other faction maintains, yet
they were accustomed to give the Tewksburys
warning of intended raids. Among other things Hegler
and McFadden told the sheepmen that John Graham

had offered a reward of $500 for the death of any of the sheep faction and $1,000 for John Tewksbury's death. Shortly after this an old man named Blevins disappeared while on the trail across Pleasant Valley to Newton's ranch. Houck, the deputy sheriff of Apache county, was himself a sheepman and allied with the Tewksburys. He went to the sheriff of the county to get warrants for the arrest of the Grahams. He was gone four days, having one hundred miles to cover, and while he was away matters came to a crisis.

From Holbrook, across the Mogollon Mountains, a band of reckless punchers connected with the Hashknife outfit came into the Tonto River Valley to help the Graham brothers. Several of these were noted gunmen. Among them was Charley Duesha, who is credited by Fred Sutton with having killed thirty-two men. This figure is probably much exaggerated. The records of few killers, as accepted by writers to-day, will bear inspection. Certainly Duesha did not kill twenty sheepmen in the Tonto Basin war, as claimed by Sutton, since the Tewksbury faction lost altogether only six men, the cattlemen being by long odds the heaviest sufferers.

The Tewksburys had learned through friends in the enemy's ranks that an attack was planned, and they moved camp five miles down the valley to a hut where they could command a view of the approach both up and down. Day and night four men kept guard on the hills above. The sheepmen were jerking beef and oiling their guns at the back door when one day five horseman rode up. Jim Tewskbury, who had been cooking dinner, stepped to the door. He noticed that the horses all carried the Hashknife brand. Tom Tucker, of the Hashknife ranch, was the leader of the five men. He fell into one of the easy, restful attitudes which the riders of the plains drop into so naturally to rest themselves.

"Is this the Tewksbury ranch?" he asked.

"No. The ranch is five miles farther down the valley," answered Jim.

"Can we get dinner here?"

"We don't keep hotel."

The two eyed each other steadily, their fingers hovering in the vicinity of their revolvers. Then Tucker turned his horse away saying, "We can go down to Vosburg's and get supper." Next moment a shot rang out. Jim Tewksbury had killed Paine, the man that rode beside Tom Tucker. He afterward claimed that Paine was drawing his six-shooter as he fired. The shooting became general in an instant. A cowboy named Bob Glasby was killed. Tom Tucker went down, wounded, behind his dead horse. He was hit five times, but emptied his revolver and lived to tell of the experience. Years later he was a law officer at Santa Fe, and "a mighty good man," according to the testimony of one of his former opponents.

Two days after this Houck reached the valley with warrants for the arrest of the Grahams, but the cattlemen naturally refused to recognize warrants served by Houck and his allies the Tewksburys. As soon as the news spread the entire country became alarmed, and when the cowboys who escaped reached their headquarters camp the cattlemen gathered their forces to return to the attack and avenge the death of their comrades. The Tewksburys wisely guessed their intentions and immediately decamped for more secure quarters. When the cowboys cautiously approached the scene of the first conflict they found only a deserted cabin. They took up the trail, and after several days' chase they located the Tewksburys on a high rocky butte where they were well fortified near a spring of water. They surrounded the camp and prepared to starve them out. After a wait of several days they left sentinels on the ground and returned to the camp for supplies and reënforcements to carry the fort. The night after the main force had departed, the Tewksburys' camp being about out of water, the defendants prepared to make a sally to the spring near at hand. Ed Tewksbury was posted on a high, flat rock overlooking the spring so that he could cover the movements of his brother Jim as he went between the camp and the spring. The moon was bright, and a man could be seen for some distance. Jim Tewksbury reached the spring without molestation. In the meantime, considerable dew had fallen, which made the trail of a man plainly visible. As he was returning he noticed that something had crossed his trail, and he suspected it had been one of the pickets of the opposition. Hanging the water canteens across his shoulders he took his rifle in both hands ready for immediate use and proceeded leisurely as before with his eyes on the trail. A sharp cry from his brother warned him to look out behind. Without turning to look he fired point-blank over his shoulder. He did not wait to discover the effect of his shot, but ran to the camp and met the information from his brother that the man who was following him went down at the crack of his gun. The Tewksburys prepared to leave camp, which they accomplished that night. It developed later that Jim Tewksbury's aim had been unerring. His shot struck his pursuer in the thigh, breaking his leg. The man bled to death before his comrades dared remove him under the guns of the Tewksburys.

There was a dance at the Central Hotel in Phoenix about this time. Among the dancers was Will Graham, a bright, care-free boy, with a merry laugh very much in evidence. Someone warned him to beware of the Tewksburys. He laughed derisively, then vaulted to his saddle and called out:

"The sheepman doesn't live that can get Will Graham."

Two weeks later his friends brought back in a soap box what the coyotes had left of the boy. The story of the killing was narrated to the writer by the man who did it. In passing it may be stated that this man, an officer of the law, killed two other men during the feud. His name is withheld for the very obvious reason that in Arizona time does not outlaw the crime of murder, but the story is told in his own words:

"One day I was coming down from Holbrook and stopped at Hegler's. I says, 'I guess I'll get supper and stop awhile.' He says, 'Get supper but don't stop—

the Grahams have been here, and I don't want no fight at the ranch. John Graham is here every evening and sometimes he comes early in the mornings.' I says, 'All right. I'll eat supper and go on.' I eat my supper and got some grub and tied it on my horse. I went out halfway between Pleasant Valley on the trail from the Graham ranch and went up on a hill and picketed my horse out and slept till daylight. At daylight I got down on the trail and got behind a tree. I left my horse on the hill. I knew John Graham would come along, and I had a warrant for him, and was going to get him. Instead of John Graham, Bill Graham come, and I didn't have a warrant for him because he was one of the younger ones, and they hadn't issued any warrant for him. I stepped out from behind the tree, and I see it was Bill with a gun in his hand. He drew a gun on me at once, and I tried to stop him—when I first see it was him, I tried to speak to him, but it was of no use. Everybody was carrying a gun them days. As he pulled his gun I turned loose and shot him. His horse whirled, and I shot three or four times—knew it was the only thing to do, for he was shooting at me as fast as he could touch the trigger. He went away and died in two days."

The Grahams took oath to avenge the death of their younger brother and imported from across the range as reckless a band of ten Texas killers as ever slapped saddle to bronco, every one of whom eventually fell victim to the wily sheepmen. The Tewksburys had wisely taken to the hills, never remaining long at one place. Their enemies trailed them to a brushy swamp, low down in the valley. The sheepmen had had a quarrel that night about where they were to camp, and John Tewksbury and Bill Jacobs had gone for their horses to move camp. Five of them were eating breakfast. Ed Tewksbury was sewing his ripped cartridge belt. While the two men were returning to camp with the horses the attacking party opened fire on them and killed both of them. There was firing all day between those in the hut and their enemies on the hill, but the Tewksburys escaped in the night by a sortie. So bitter was the feeling that the Texans allowed the bodies of their victims to be devoured by hogs.

Three weeks later the feudists met again just below John Tewksbury's home on Cherry Creek, and this time it was still the cattlemen that were the attackers. It was early morning, and some of the sheepmen were still dozing in their blankets when the cowpunchers swept in on them. Jim Roberts and Jim Tewksbury turned over in their blankets and began to shoot. A man named Middleton was killed by them, and one Ellenwood badly wounded. The Grahams were driven back and retreated with their dead and wounded.

So the war ran on until there remained alive but one Graham. Years passed, and the feud appeared to have died out, for John Graham had moved to Tempe and had apparently given up the fight. Then on July 13, 1892, John Graham signed his own death warrant. He went back to Tonto Basin, rounded up his cattle, and drove them away. Many people believe he might be living to this day had he not foolishly boasted of his exploit. He insinuated that Tewksbury had been afraid to attack him. Six weeks later, while driving to Tempe with a load of grain from his home near the Buttes, Graham was shot close to the Cummings ranch. He lived till next morning and told Charlie Duesha and others that Ed Tewksbury and John Rhodes were the assassins.

Rhodes, who had married the widow of John Tewksbury and had been identified with that faction ever since the trouble began to brew, was taken to Phoenix and tried. The testimony was all very conflicting. Many of the witnesses swore positively to seeing Rhodes near the Cummings ranch on the morning of the killing in company with a man who wore a scarlet ribbon tied round a white sombrero. As many swore to an alibi for him. He was eventually acquitted. As the trial progressed the widow of Graham, a woman of strong feeling, convinced as the testimony piled high against him that her husband's murderer sat before her, drew a .44 calibre revolver and leaped toward Rhodes. Her father caught her arm, and the shots went wild. Rhodes, after his acquittal, was guarded out of town by a host of armed friends.

Tewksbury was tried later. The scarlet ribbon round the white sombrero convicted him. He was granted a new trial and released on bail. The case against him was finally dropped. He was a man of iron nerve, of wonderful physique, and a dead shot.

It is said that his great rifle was so heavy that no other man in the valley could handle it.

John Rhodes I knew personally. He became a respected cattleman, a school trustee, and one very well thought of by his neighbours. It is hard to believe that jovial, warm-hearted Rhodes, the best cowman in Pinal County, could be guilty of a cowardly assassination. Years later the writer rode on the round-up with him in Pinal County, and the evidence of all his fellows is that Rhodes was "a man to tie to." He was a man of splendid physique and threw the longest rope of any cowboy I ever knew. It was characteristic, however, of nearly all the men engaged in this feud that they were in general good citizens in a rough way. Even the Tewksburys were usually quiet men of a friendly and generous disposition, though they were wild and unmanageable when in drink.

Pleasant Valley lies under the foothills of the Mogollon Ridge, and it was here in the rough country back of the fine rolling pasturage that the main fights occurred. It is a beautiful country, having many springs and streams of water. But from the earliest days it carried a record of blood. The first three white men that ever went into the valley quarrelled about the division of their land, and two of them killed the third. Its history is so dark that for long the valley was empty of settlers.

CARRYING LAW INTO THE MESQUITE

Captain Burton Mossman of the Arizona Rangers

"SHOTGUN" Smith had just been acquitted by a jury of his peers of the crime of cattle rustling and was consequently celebrating the occasion by "tanking up," as he himself would phrase it, with a company of choice friends at the Holbrook hotel bar. His tongue was in that state of eloquence common to the bad man when he drinks. He was extemporizing a poem in profanity. It was in blank verse, and the subject of it was the things he would do to one Mossman when he came across him. For Burton Mossman, superintendent of the Aztec Cattle Company, commonly known as the Hashknife outfit, had sought and found the evidence that might have convicted him before a less prejudiced jury.

At this moment, as fate would have it, enter Mossman upon the stage of action. The barkeeper warned him of the situation by a lift of the eyebrow, and Mossman could easily have stepped out of the front room without being observed by those behind. Another man probably would have done this, but that is not Mossman's way. He sauntered into the barroom, cool and easy and debonair, nodded coolly, and ordered a drink. Shotgun's hand stole back to his belt. The superintendent of the Aztec Cattle Company looked at him out of those steel-gray eyes of his. "I wouldn't if I were you, Shotgun," he said quietly. Shotgun's eyes fell; his hand dropped from the coveted revolver handle. There was something compelling about this little man's quiet manner that induced a change of mind on his part. He suddenly remembered an engagement elsewhere.

A few years prior to this some of the big cattlemen thought of going out of the business. Mormon and Gentile rustlers and Mexican border thieves were stealing and branding their cattle by hundreds. Legal convictions were apparently impossible because of the lack of absolute evidence in each individual case. Even if a calf was recognized as belonging to a certain outfit, the rustler had but to plead that he had branded it by mistake: "I didn't know the calf, but it sure was following my cow." Up to the time that Burton Mossman went in as superintendent of the Aztec Cattle Company no conviction for cattle stealing had been obtained by them for fourteen years. Within ten months of his incumbency Mossman had twelve miscreants landed in the penitentiary under conviction of cattle stealing. He always took the field himself with his deputies and worked up the case personally. The result was that he was able to secure evidence that resulted in seriously crippling the business of the desperadoes of Navajo and Apache counties.

Mossman's life was threatened again and again, and he was in a dozen serious affrays. On March 17, 1899, in company with a deputy sheriff he had a fight with the Baca gang of Mexicans in which the two Americans drove away the gang of five and captured one of them. The shooting was so close that Mossman's bridle rein was divided in his hand. The gang returned for reënforcements, while Mossman and the deputy hurried their prisoner away, with his feet tied under a horse, to the nearest town. They travelled by day, and stood guard over him for two nights until they reached the county seat, sixty-five miles away, just twenty-five minutes ahead of the bloodthirsty troop of Mexican bandits.

"Gone to Texas!" Away back in the '60's this expression held a sinister meaning. To use it of a man was to imply that he was at outs with the law. But the forward-lapping tide of civilization has changed all that, and one mighty factor in the change was that stalwart little band of men known as the Texas Rangers. A little later than the '60's something of this same cloud hung over Arizona's clear title to a claim as a law-abiding community. From Austin and San Antonio to Abilene, from Abilene to Dodge City—from this "worst town on earth" westward to Las Vegas and Santa Fe, and from thence to the virgin Southwest of Tucson and Tombstone, a crooked line of this sporadic frontier lawlessness took its way. In each of these places the bad man found his habitat for the time, until encroaching civilization drove him to new pastures.

By special reasons of locality, frontier conditions prevailed longer in Arizona than elsewhere. This was due to the facts that it is a cattle country with its consequent temptations to rustling, that the population was sparse, and that it was near the Mexican line. At any rate—for long, murderers and desperadoes infested the headwaters of the San Francisco, Salt, and Black rivers among the almost inaccessible mountain wilds. It was to meet this condition of affairs that the second Arizona territorial legislature authorized Governor Murphy to organize a company of Rangers. Of this company Mr. Burton Mossman was selected to be the captain. He accepted the appointment purely out of a sense of duty and adventure, since the pay attached to the post was five dollars a month less than his chief clerk was receiving at the time.

Burton Mossman was one of the most picturesque characters in Arizona, but at first glance he did not look the part. He was then a well-groomed little fellow, who fell easily into graceful attitudes and gave the impression of being a typical languid club man rather than a frontiersman of unusual nerve and daring. This was the first thought, but presently you noticed that there was endurance in his well-knit frame and that his cold gray eye was like steel. His easy, imperturbable manner together with his instinctively alert mind and his keen knowledge of character combined to make him a most formidable poker player. One saw him rake in a five-hundred-dollar jack pot without the flicker of an eyelid, after a remarkably cool play. Governor Murphy showed judgment of men when he chose Burton Mossman to be captain of the Rangers.

The work assigned to these Rangers was an arduous and a dangerous one. For many years sheriffs' officers and Vigilantes had found themselves entirely unable to cope with the lawless bands which made their headquarters in the bad lands. But the condition of affairs had grown unendurable. The temerity of the outlaws was not only a scourge to the community, but a menace to the good name of the Territory. No man's sheep or cattle were safe from the raids of the organized bands of outlaws, who would sweep down on a range, drive away the cattle, and reach the mountain fastnesses long before the posse could be organized for pursuit. Raids and murders had become so common that they were scarcely noted. There were a dozen bands of these murderous horse and cattle thieves, at the head of which were such men as Bill Smith, the notorious Augustine Chacon, commonly called "Pelelo," and the train robber, Burt Alvord. Yet within a year of the time of its organization this little band of Rangers, consisting of a captain, a sergeant, and twelve privates, had largely cleared the territory of hundreds of bad characters. Many of them had paid for their lawlessness with their lives and the rest had been driven across the line into Mexico.

The Rangers' work was so effective that it is a matter of surprise to those who understand the conditions under which they have operated. Captain

Mossman's plan was to keep the men always armed, mounted, and equipped, so that they might be ready to get right after their men as soon as word came in from the cattle camps that rustlers or raiders had been at work. The Rangers were divided into little squads and sent out either alone or in pairs to scout along the borders or upon some definite detail. In many cases they went hundreds of miles into territory where they were not known at all. For weeks and even for months no news was heard of them, until some day the Ranger sent a report to headquarters that his man was landed in prison with enough evidence to convict him. The Rangers were recruited from old cowboys, and from the ranks of Roosevelt's Rough Riders. They had to be able to rope and ride anything on four legs, as their horses might be killed and remounts were at times absolutely necessary. Especially quick work was required in heading fugitives from the border. A crime was reported, the Ranger slapped on the saddle and was away. To the credit of the Ranger it may be said that nine times out of ten he brought back his man, dead or alive.

Shortly after the organization of the Rangers the Tucumcara band of outlaws led by Bill Daniels robbed the postoffice and store near Fort Sumner, held up the men about the station, and killed a boy who stood there with his hands up. They were followed a hundred miles by the United States territorial officials across the Arizona lines. Before they had been in Arizona a week the Arizona

Rangers had captured four of them near the head-waters of the Blue River, securing from them an arsenal of arms, more than a thousand rounds of ammunition, wire pincers to cut fences, and other paraphernalia. In their mountain fastnesses they were prepared to stand a long siege, but Mossman's dashing Rangers rushed in on them and took them hotfoot. Witt Neil and one Roberts were taken in bed, two more were ambushed, and Sam Bass was followed across the Mexican line and secured.

Scarcely a month had passed before word reached Captain Mossman of a serious reverse to his troops. A few of them had been following the notorious Bill Smith gang and had come on them suddenly. A long running fight through the mesquite and chaparral ensued. Finally Bill Smith proposed to surrender and came forward without a gun. Bill Maxwell and Carlos Tefio, both of whom were noted for their extreme courage, stepped forward to indicate where the gang might lay down their arms. Smith pretended to stumble behind a stump, seized a rifle which he had hidden there, and treacherously murdered Maxwell. A moment later Tefio also was shot through the bow-els. He knew the wound was mortal, but shot twelve times from his tracks before he fell—then crawled back to his horse and died. For many hours the fight was at the very close range of 125 yards, but in the darkness of the following night the outlaws made their escape.

Captain Mossman flung a saddle on his bronco and hurried to the scene of action. With him were two expert San Carlos Apache Indian trailers named "Kid" and "Josh."[1]

For twenty-two days Mossman and his guides followed the trail of Smith. The weather was at the worst. It rained repeatedly and obliterated the trail, and a snowstorm came up and impeded the pursuers. The trail was found again and resumed. For eight days the outlaws were pressed so close that they had to wander horseless in the mountain fastnesses. Several of them were wounded. But from the McKean ranch they secured remounts and again escaped. In many places the trail was far too rough to follow on horseback, but the indefatigable pursuers never despaired. Finally, despite his exertions, Captain Mossman was beaten, for a second snowstorm hid the trail for days and enabled the bandits to cross the line into New Mexico. But they had had enough of Arizona and her Rangers and have since given them a clear berth.

Two of the most signal feats in which Captain Mossman was individually concerned were the running down at different times of the notorious Mexican bandits Salivaras and Chacon. The first of these cut-throats had murdered the superintendent of the Calico mines, while the latter was transporting gold across the mountains to pay off his men. Salivaras took to the cactus-covered desert and struck far across it to a water hole along an unfrequented trail known to but few. His horse gave out and died at Paradise Valley, and the highwayman followed the

[1]See the story of "The 'Apache Kid.'"

novel procedure of burying himself up to the chin in mud with his booty beneath him and a bunch of Spanish bayonet in front to conceal his head. Soon Mossman came up and his dogs went straight to the outlaw, who crawled from his hole and opened fire. His bullet got Mossman in the side, but on the return shot the captain of the Rangers hit Salivaras in the breast and ended his career.

Augustine Chacon was the leader of the worst gang of outlaws that ever infested the border. His stronghold was in the Sierra Madres mountains, and from it he sallied to ride on the raids that terrorized the settlers. He had a reputed record of killing twenty-eight persons, and doubtless many unknown victims had fallen by his rifle.

John Slaughter, famous sheriff of Cochise County, a quiet little cattleman with a nerve of steel, had had his troubles with Chacon. The outlaw had threatened to kill him, and Slaughter had countered by attempting to arrest him in Tombstone. On this occasion an accident saved the life of Chacon. He fell over a guy wire just as the fighting sheriff's bullets flew past him in the darkness.

Burt Alvord, one of Slaughter's cowboys, was with his boss at the time, and strangely enough it was later Alvord, by this time graduated into a train robber himself, who acted as a decoy on behalf of Mossman.

But many years of deviltry by Chacon passed in the interval between the two adventures.

In 1896 Chacon's gang robbed a store near Morenci,

cut the storekeeper to pieces with knives, and got away, followed by a sheriff's posse. In the fight that ensued Chacon killed Pablo Salcido, a deputy sheriff, while under a flag of truce. The deed was witnessed by the whole posse, but though two of Chacon's gang were killed he himself escaped for the moment. Shot through the body shortly afterward, he was captured, convicted, and sentenced to be hung. Influential friends worked hard for him and carried the case to the Supreme Court, which reaffirmed the decision of the lower court. Six days before the time set for his hanging, with the connivance of a woman, Chacon broke jail and crossed the line into Mexico. Here he joined Mexican border guards for a year and a half, when he had a difficulty with another soldier and deserted. He resumed with increased ferocity his career of highway robbery and murder, flitting to and fro across the Arizona-Mexican line at his convenience. On one occasion he passed within a mile or two of Solomonville, where the sentence of death was still hanging over his head, and went up Eagle Creek into the mountain gorges. Here he killed two prospectors and for two weeks was followed by the sheriff's posses, but again reached and passed the line in safety. From now on he crossed to and fro continually to steal horses and pursue his vocation of murder.

At this time Burt Alvord, the leader of the band of train robbers who held up the Southern Pacific train at Sonora, was living as a fugitive in Mexico. He had escaped from the Tombstone jail in 1899 and was for three years an outlaw in the brush while his fellow train robbers were serving long terms in the penitentiary. Mossman heard indirectly of Alvord's whereabouts through Sheriff Tom Turner of Santa Cruz and Del Lewis of Cochise County. These two men, armed with extradition papers obtained from the governor of Sonora, had crossed and attempted Alvord's capture. Warned by local officers of their approach, Alvord had escaped by two hours' start in the mountains. Mossman knew Alvord had worked with Chacon on some of his raids and conceived the idea of using Alvord as a stool pigeon. The ranger captain went alone into Minas Pritas, where he secured a four-horse team and drove to San José de Pima. There he got a saddle horse and took to the brush for days in the hope of running on the camp of Alvord. At last he found the man at a lonely adobe hut on a high range overlooking the country. When Captain Mossman rode up, quite unarmed, Alvord was standing alone outside the hut. Inside, his men were gambling and playing cards. Mossman had never seen the outlaw but recognized him by his pictures.

"I suppose I am talking to the noted bandit, Burt Alvord," said Captain Mossman, by way of beginning the conversation.

Alvord laughed and nodded: "Who are you?"

"My name is Mossman. I am the captain of the Arizona Rangers."

"The devil you are!" Alvord's keen eye ranged the mesquite-covered hill in search of hidden troops, and instinctively his hand went to his hip.

It was Mossman's turn to laugh, and he did it

easily and naturally. "Oh, I am not such a fool as to come looking for you this way if my visit were not friendly. I am alone and in your power. I want to talk with you, but as I am hungry, suppose you feed me first."

Mossman stayed twenty-four hours with Burt Alvord, as his guest. He knew that at any moment the train robber might become suspicious and shoot him down like a dog, but he manifested no nervousness even though he was afraid that the sudden appearance of the Mexican Rangers with Sheriff Turner might ring his death knell. Alvord was tired of the hard life he had been living in the brush, and before Mossman left him the outlaw had agreed to find Chacon and induce him to cross the line into the United States. Alvord wanted somebody to act as his messenger to Mossman, and at his suggestion Billy Stiles, who was one of the Southern Pacific train robbers in Alvord's gang, was chosen. Stiles had given evidence which secured the conviction of his confederates and had afterward joined the Arizona Rangers.

It was on April 22, 1902, that Mossman first met Alvord; but the train robber did not run across Chacon before July. Then Alvord had to accompany Chacon down to the Yaqui with some stolen horses. Finally they came back, Stiles having already joined them. Alvord sent Stiles ahead to notify Captain Mossman of their approach with this message:

In nine days meet us twenty-five miles within the Mexican line at the Socorro Mountain spring, joining us as a confederate.

Captain Mossman and Stiles rode to the spring, but missing Alvord and Chacon came back to the American side. They had ridden all night and loafed the day away in the chaparral. At nightfall Mossman sent Stiles forward across the line to an adobe hut where Alvord's wife lived, thinking that possibly the man might be there. On the way there Stiles met the two outlaws and returned with them to a barbed-wire fence which separates the American from the Mexican side. There they met Mossman. After some parley the fence was cut and the Ranger captain joined them on the Mexican side. Burt Alvord introduced Mossman as an outlaw desirous of joining their gang, and Chacon was apparently satisfied. Together they planned to rustle a bunch of horses from Greene's pasture, which was seven miles on the American side.

The four men rode down the line for several miles, then crossed at Greene's ranch. The night had fallen black with no moon, and they found it too dark to rob the pasture. They made a fire of greasewood and camped beside it. One may conceive that even Mossman's jaunty nerves must have been strained to the uttermost during that night. He was in a situation the most uncertain, for it was entirely within the possibilities that he might be the victim of a ruse and that the three bandits would murder him in his sleep. Before daybreak Alvord tiptoed across to where Mossman lay and announced that he was going to leave him.

"I brought Chacon to you, but you don't seem

able to take him. I've done my share, and I don't want him to suspect me. Remember that if you take him you have promised that the reward shall go to me, and that you'll stand by me at my trial if I surrender. You sure want to be mighty careful, or he'll kill you. So long."

Mossman nodded, and Alvord stealthily departed. When Chacon woke and found that Alvord was not of the party his suspicions at once were aroused. Stiles suggested that they then go after the Greene ranch horses, but Chacon said they had better eat breakfast first. During breakfast time he said scarcely a word, but his suspicions grew more active. While Stiles and Mossman made the fire and fried the bacon on the end of a stick he sat back and lowered at Mossman. His furtive eyes never left the Ranger's face. Every move was watched with a lynxlike intensity.

The Ranger captain now realized that getting the drop on his man would be no easy matter. His rifle lay a few yards from the fire, but he never wandered from it more than two or three paces. He, too, had grown suspicious, knowing well that Chacon was meditating sending a bullet through his heart if opportunity offered. Chacon's wariness was by no means a conviction that treachery was meant him, but it would take a great deal less than conviction to make the Mexican murderer shoot. After breakfast Chacon announced decisively that he would go no further in the business. Mossman shrugged his shoulders and said it didn't matter to him. As Chacon understood

English, Mossman had no chance to converse with Stiles privately, and presently the bandit announced that he was going back across the line.

Mossman knew the moment for action had come. Chacon and Stiles were squatting side by side smoking cigarettes. The Ranger captain sauntered forward and asked Chacon for one, saying that he always liked those Mexican cigarettes. He then backed to the fire, stooped, and with his left hand picked up a glowing juniper branch. This he changed to his right hand and lighted the cigarette, his eyes still on Chacon. He came back toward the two men, puffing the smoke carelessly. When it was well lighted he dropped the juniper stick, his hand falling to his side; then as he raised his hand, with the same movement—like a flash—his revolver came out. Chacon was covered.

"Hands up, Chacon."

Chacon's face never quivered. "Is this a joke?" he asked.

"No. Throw your hands up or you're a dead man."

Chacon sparred for time. "I don't see as it makes any difference after he is dead whether a man's hands are up or down. You're going to kill me anyway. Why don't you shoot?"

Mossman had been dubious of Stiles. He was afraid that the latter would side with the winning man. If he secured Chacon he knew the Ranger would remain true, but if the cards went against him he was not to be relied upon. Mossman's move then had the additional advantage of covering Stiles, too, if anything went wrong.

Chacon's eyes never wavered from those of Mossman, but by burning concentration he attempted to make the latter shift his gaze for just one instant. The tenth part of a second would have been long enough for he was the quickest man on the frontier with a gun. But in Mossman he met his match. The Ranger chief ordered Stiles to disarm him, and from the lining of his coat Stiles ripped a pair of handcuffs and slipped them on the bandit. Immediately the three men headed toward the railroad. Several times Chacon attempted to throw himself from his horse.

"I'll drag you by your neck to the railroad," Mossman told him.

Stiles led the way followed by Chacon, while Mossman touched up his horse from behind. Mossman boarded the train with him, took him to Benson, and delivered him to the sheriff. He was hanged at Solomonville. The man died game, showing the coolest daring on the scaffold. He laughed and joked with his executioners, smoked a cigarette without a tremor, and was apparently unconcerned. Just before his arms were pinioned he waved a jaunty hand and cried, "*Adios, amigo.*"

Mossman resigned his commission as captain of the Rangers about this time, and Lieutenant Thomas Rynning of Troop B, Roosevelt's Rough Riders, was appointed by Governor Brodie to succeed him. It is sufficient to say of Captain Rynning that while his work was not so dramatic as Mossman's it was just as soldierly and effective. He continued the policy begun by the former, of hunting thieves and murderers with such steady continuity that, one after another, they found their business unprofitable.

When I last heard of them Mossman was a cattleman at Roswell, New Mexico, and Rynning was in charge of the Arizona State Penitentiary at Florence.

THE HUNTING OF HARRY
TRACY[1]

The Most Thrilling Man Hunt of Recent
Western History

No HALO of romance hangs over the head of Harry
Tracy. He does not belong to the old West. He had
no Bret Harte complex. There is no chance that
blended fact and fiction will make of his life a legend.
He was a criminal at heart, a cold-blooded killing
machine. But it must be admitted that in his own
line he was preëminent.

The most thrilling man hunt America has ever
known began on the morning of June 9, 1902, at the
gates of the Oregon Penitentiary, and continued
with unabated vigour until August 5th. Early on
June 9th Harry Tracy, murderer and convicted
burglar, assisted by his partner, David Merrill,
escaped from prison after killing three guards, wounding a fourth, and shattering the leg of another prisoner
who attempted to wrest from him the rifle with which
he was armed. For nearly two months this keen-eyed,
resourceful, and desperate outlaw wrote in blood the
most thrilling melodrama ever enacted in real life.

---

[1]Portions of this story were first used by the *Wide World Magazine*.

No "penny dreadful" ever bristled with such fascinating impossibilities; no character in fiction ever combined with such wonderful nerve and daring so much shrewdness, dogged determination, deadly skill with weapons, and knowledge of human nature as was displayed by the outlaw Tracy. To say that not once, during the months in which he was hunted by hundreds of armed men and by bloodhounds, did he show the white feather, or even the slightest excitement, is to tell but a small part of the truth. Many men on the Western frontier might have emulated his coolness and nerve, but not one of them could have paralleled his smiling audacity, his contempt for fearful odds, the skill with which he eluded his pursuers, and the unfailing accuracy with which he executed his carefully planned manoeuvres. Whenever the arm of the law was stretched forth to gather him in, Tracy, like a tiger at bay, showed his teeth and bit so suddenly and so fearfully that brave men stood aghast. His fight for liberty was the most desperate in the criminal annals of America. The exploits of the famous Jesse James gang are not to be compared with the lurid escape and subsequent pursuit of Harry Tracy across hundreds of miles of unfriendly country. For daring, fertility of resource, and cold-blooded nerve his fight for liberty against almost impossible numbers is without a parallel. Hunted by thousands of armed men, with a reward of $8,000 on his head, dead or alive, Tracy for months defied capture, leaving dead and wounded men behind him whenever he was hard pressed.

On June 9, 1902, the foundry gang of prisoners at the Salem (Oregon) Penitentiary was marched to its work as usual by Guards Girard and Ferrell. The convicts were counted in and announced as all present by Girard. While the words were still on his lips a rifle shot echoed through the yard, and Ferrell fell forward with a cry of agony. He had been killed by Harry Tracy, a convict, who had already murdered two men in Colorado and was serving a twenty-years' sentence for burglary along with an accomplice named David Merrill. Tracy, seconded by his partner in crime, now turned upon the other guards and began shooting. A life prisoner, Ingram by name, leaped upon Tracy with the intention of disarming him, but was immediately shot down by Merrill. In the confusion the two desperate men scaled the prison walls by means of a ladder which they found near at hand. Once over they turned their attention to the fence guards. S. R. Jones, patrolling the northwest corner of the stockade, fell, pierced by two bullets. Another guard, Duncan Ross, was wounded. Guard Tiffany emptied his rifle at the men but failed to hit his mark. He was himself wounded and fell from the wall to the ground, where he was picked up by the two escaping prisoners, who calmly used him as a shield while they retreated to the woods. At the edge of the forest they shot him, took his rifle, and disappeared into the underbrush.

Tracy and Merrill were well armed with short Winchesters, which it is thought must have been secretly supplied to them by sympathizers who visited the prison in the guise of excursionists. They had already killed three men in order to escape, and while at liberty were a menace to the community. So an urgent call was sent for assistance. Sheriff Durbin, with a heavily armed posse, immediately answered the telephone message sent him, and appeared at the prison to assist Superintendent Lee, of the penitentiary, in recapturing the escaped convicts.

The two criminals, however, managed to elude pursuit during the whole day, and under cover of night passed through Salem. Here they held up a man named J. W. Stewart, made him disrobe, and took his clothing. Later an expressman named Welch discarded, at their orders, an overcoat and a pair of overalls; and the stable of one Felix Labaucher furnished them with two fast horses. One notable fact in the escape of the desperado Tracy is the fear which he somehow managed to instil into the minds of the hardy frontiersmen among whom he lived for the next two months, and which stood him in good stead on many occasions when he was hard pressed.

Heavily armed, in citizens' clothing, and mounted on good horses, the convicts were now prepared to make a stubborn fight for liberty. No more dangerous criminal than Tracy, in fact, was ever turned loose upon a community. He was a dead shot and did not know what fear meant.

Bloodhounds sent down from the Washington State Penitentiary followed the scent of the fugitives for some time, but finally lost it. The pair were seen next morning at Brooks, a station on the Southern

Pacific Railway eight miles north of Salem. During the night they had found it necessary to get rid of their horses. On June 11th the two men were surrounded by a posse of fifty men near Gervais. They were still on the line of the Southern Pacific and were headed north for the State of Washington via Portland. The couple were known to be exceedingly well armed, for during the night they had had the audacity to hold up two of the pursuing posse and relieve them of their weapons! Before noon a hundred men surrounded the woods in which the men lurked. Every man within a radius of ten miles who possessed a gun was summoned to join the posse, and Company F of the Oregon State National Guards also arrived upon the scene. A complete cordon surrounded the apparently doomed men, but during the night the two desperadoes slipped silently through the lines and escaped.

They were next seen at the house of Mrs. Akers, where they forced the farmer's wife to prepare them a good breakfast. After they had gone the farmer telephoned to Sheriff Durbin, who came on at once with his posse and the bloodhounds.

The escaped prisoners pressed forward to Clackamas County, where Sheriff Cook with a posse and three companies of militia took up the chase. As they continued north the desperadoes lived on the country, holding up farms for food and horses as they travelled. They always boldly announced who they were. A dozen times they were shot at, several times they were surrounded, and once Tracy fired and winged one of his pursuers. The reward for the capture of the convicts was doubled, and doubled again, and public excitement grew intense. For five days the sheriff and his posse continued the chase, and then gave up, weary and discouraged.

Meanwhile, Tracy had forced a farmer at the muzzle of his revolver to row him and his companion across the Columbia River into Washington. They dined at the house of a farmer named Peedy, whom they tied and gagged before leaving. Sheriff Marsh, of Clarke County, with a very large force, took up the chase with energy. A four-cornered duel took place between the fugitives and two of the posse who came in touch with them, but the convicts again escaped unhurt. For some days after this episode their trail was completely lost.

It was on July 2d that Tracy reappeared to enact the most stirring scenes of his melodramatic career. He had been heading for the Puget Sound country, and after holding up a farmer or two for practice he modestly decided to honour the city of Seattle with a visit. It was early morning, and the sun was just breaking through the mist and fog that hung over South Bay, near Olympia, the state capital, when a man entered the tent of an oyster fishery company and ordered Mr. Horatio Alling, the manager, and his two men to furnish him a meal.

"I'm Tracy, the convict," said the stranger. "I want something to eat right away. Be quiet, raise no fuss, and I won't harm you."

A launch lay at anchor near the tent, and Tracy

ordered one of the men to call her captain to break-fast. The convict waited coolly till Captain Clark and his son had finished breakfast and then ordered Clark to get up steam at once, as he desired to go to Seattle. Before leaving he tied Mr. Alling and the cook hand and foot and helped himself to any clothes that took his fancy.

From 1894 till 1898 I had lived near Seattle and at this time I was back there visiting my parents Alling had been a very close friend of mine, and his adventure with Tracy stimulated my already keen interest in the chase. Later, in the capacity of a news-paper correspondent, I saw a good deal of the men who had charge of the capture of the outlaw and was at one time with the posse (entirely as a pacifist) which operated near Bothell.

During the launch ride to Seattle Tracy remained at one end of the little cabin, his gun resting in his lap ready for use in case any of the actions of his crew appeared to him suspicious. For twelve hours the bandit was complete master of the situation. He was easy, unconcerned, and debonair, ready to joke and to laugh with his unwilling servants, but his steely eyes never relaxed their vigilance for a moment. Someone asked him where his partner Merrill was.

Tracy's face set hard.

"I killed him," he answered quietly.

"Killed him?" reiterated his questioner, in sur-prise.

"Yes, I killed him. He had no nerve and he was a traitor. I read in the Portland papers after our escape that it was due to information from Merrill that I was caught in the first place—that time I stole the engine and was knocked senseless by a glancing shot. Merrill had told them where they could find me. Then, too, he was a coward, always ready to bolt. He was no good. The man was frightened to death all the time. It made me angry when the papers gave him half the credit for our escape. I told him he was a coward, and he got huffy. Then we decided to fight a duel when we were near Chehalis. We were to start, back to back, and walk ten paces each, then wheel round and begin firing. He haggled so in arranging the terms that I knew he meant to play false. I couldn't trust him, so when I had taken eight steps I fired over my shoulder. I hit him in the back. The first shot did not finish him, so I shot again. He only got what he deserved. The fellow meant to kill me treacherously and steal out of the country through the big timber, leaving my dead body among the leaves."

The finding of Merrill's body two weeks later proved the truth of Tracy's treachery toward his companion. He had evidently found that the other man was losing his nerve, and had got rid of him to save further trouble.

All day Tracy displayed the greatest carelessness in regard to human life. At one time he desired the captain of the launch to run in close to McNeil's Island, where a government military prison is located, in order that he might get a pot shot at one of the guards. During the day he dozed slightly once or twice, but, as his rifle was across his lap and the slightest movement awakened him, the crew dared not interfere with him. At Meadow Point, near the city of Seattle, Tracy finished his yachting trip, tied the captain and crew up, and went ashore, forcing one of the terrified men to accompany him as a guide. The ascendancy this man acquired over everybody he met is remarkable.

The outlaw headed toward the north end of Lake Washington and was recognized more than once before he reached Bothell. Here he lay hidden till morning in the dense brush and secured some much-needed sleep. It was raining hard, but there is no doubt that the escaped convict found shelter from the storm under some big logs. Meanwhile, Seattle was full of wild rumours about Tracy. Every stray tramp was an object of suspicion, and the greatest excitement prevailed among people. Before night the excitement had increased tenfold. Harry Tracy, it was reported, had come into touch with two posses, had engaged in battle with them, killed three officers and wounded one, and had himself escaped unhurt!

Persistent reports came to the city of Tracy's presence near Bothell. It was said that he was surrounded in a brickyard; that he had several times been definitely identified by men who saw him skulking in the heavy timber. Sheriff Cudihee, of King County, a fearless and efficient officer who had a good record for running down criminals, at once ordered posses to the scene and hastened there himself. It may be stated in passing that from that moment to the time of Tracy's death Sheriff Cudihee hung doggedly to the trail of the flying bandit. Other sheriffs took up the hunt and dropped it when the convict had passed out of their bailiwicks, but Cudihee alone followed him like a bloodhound wherever he went, until the question of Tracy's escape or capture came to be a personal issue between Edward Cudihee and Harry Tracy, two of the most fearless and determined men that ever carried a gun.

At Bothell the posse separated, and every road was guarded. Two officials from Everett, several from Seattle, and Mr. Louie B. Sefrit, a reporter for the Seattle *Times*, started down the road toward Pontiac, part of them following the railway track and part the wagon road. About a hundred yards southeast of where the railroad track and the wagon road cross again there were two small cabins standing in a yard which was much overgrown with grass, weeds, and old tree stumps. Three men, named Williams, Brewer, and Nelson, jumped through a wire fence and started toward the cabins, while the others went down the track to examine the cabins from that side. Said one Raymond to Sefrit, the reporter:

"I believe Tracy is in that yard."

Sefrit answered that he thought so, too, for the grass had been freshly beaten down. He pointed to a black stump some five yards in front of him. Like all tree stumps in the Puget Sound country, it had been partly burned.

"That's exactly where I believe he is," said Raymond. "Let's———"

He never finished the sentence. From behind the stump arose Tracy himself, his rifle at his shoulder. There came a flash, and Anderson, one of the deputies, fell. Still another spit of flame belched from the rifle, and Raymond fell back with a stifled cry. He was quite dead before help reached him. Sefrit took a shot at the desperado with a Colt's revolver, whereupon Tracy wheeled and let drive at him. Sefrit, realizing that he was in an exposed position, fell as if shot. The outlaw fired again at him, then waited watchfully to make sure he had killed his man. A bunch of grass lay between Sefrit's head and Tracy, but the reporter could see the convict crouching behind the stump and knew that the slightest movement meant death. So for some minutes the *Times* reporter lay there in an agony of suspense, expecting every moment to feel a bullet tearing through his breast. Then Tracy slowly began to back away in the drenching rain. Two more shots rang out, and Jack Williams, who had been coming forward from the rear, fell, desperately wounded.

Tracy scudded away in the thick underbrush, and half a mile from the scene of battle relieved a rancher of a horse he was riding. This he presently discarded, impressing into his service a farmer named Louis Johnson, with his wagon. He forced the farmer to drive him to Fremont, which is a suburb of Seattle. By this time the escaped convict was very hungry. He made Johnson hitch his team to the fence outside the home of Mrs. R. H. Van Horn and then invited himself to dinner. Mrs. Van Horn at once recognized Tracy from his published photograph.

"What do you want?" she asked.

"Food, madam, and clothing," returned the urbane murderer. It chanced that there was a man named Butterfield in the house, and from him Tracy coolly took the dry clothing which he wore. Being in a good humour, the bandit dropped into the kitchen and conversed with Mrs. Van Horn while she prepared his meal for him.

"I have never 'held up' a lady before," he explained, while eating the food. "I don't want to have to tie you when I leave. Will you promise not to say anything about my having been here?"

"For to-night I will—but not to-morrow morning," answered the plucky little woman.

"That will be all right," said Tracy; "I'll be far enough away by then. I want to tell you, madam, that I haven't enjoyed a meal so much in three years." He then mentioned his "yachting trip," as he called it, from Olympia to Seattle.

At eight-thirty o'clock a knock came at the door. Mr. Butterfield answered it and said that it was the grocery boy.

"If you tell him anything it will mean death to the men here," Tracy told Mrs. Van Horn significantly, as she went to give her orders to the boy.

Nevertheless, she took occasion to nod her head toward the door and whisper the one word "Tracy" to the boy. He understood, and two minutes later was lashing his horse along the road toward Fremont. When Tracy rose to depart an hour later Sheriff Cudihee lay in ambush within six feet of the Johnson wagon.

Tracy thanked Mrs. Van Horn for his meal in courteous fashion, then stepped down the path to the road with Butterfield and Johnson on either side of him. Meanwhile, the vigilant Sheriff Cudihee lay in wait for his man near the wagon. As Tracy sauntered down the path the sheriff of King County covered him every inch of the way with his Winchester. There was just a shadow of doubt in his mind as to which of the three was the man he wanted. He decided to wait until the outlaw climbed into the wagon.

Suddenly out of the darkness rushed Police Officer Breece, Mr. J. I. McKnight, and Game Warden Neil Rawley. Breece covered the convict with his rifle from a distance of about ten yards and cried, "Throw down that gun, Tracy!"

The desperado wheeled and fired point-blank. Breece fell over, a dead man. Twice more the convict fired, this time at Rawley, and the game warden went to the ground mortally wounded. Tracy dashed through the fence and made for the woods. The sheriff levelled his rifle and fired twice at the disappearing convict, but owing to the darkness neither shot took effect. Harry Tracy, burglar, outlaw, and murderer, had again broken through the death trap that had been prepared for him. Had it not been for the recklessness of interfering officials Cudihee would undoubtedly have caught or killed his man.

With the curious mania which he had for continually doubling on his tracks Tracy again headed for Bothell, near which point he held up Farmer Fisher for clothes and provisions. Cornered in a strip of country not twenty miles square, in the midst of which was a city of one hundred and twenty thousand population, though three bodies lay in the county morgue to attest his unerring skill and others lay wounded near to death in the hospitals, yet Harry Tracy still roamed the country like an Apache, uninjured and untamable. Whenever men bearded him he left a trail of blood behind him in his relentless flight. He himself condoned his crimes because, as he said, he killed to satisfy no lust for blood but simply to keep his cherished liberty.

In order to understand how one fearless man was able for so long a time to defy the law, the nature of the country must be considered. The Puget Sound country was at that time the most densely timbered on earth. The underbrush is very heavy, and a rank growth of ferns some four feet high covers the ground like a carpet. A man might slip into the ferns and remain hidden for months within a dozen yards of the roadside provided the food question were eliminated. The one thing that Tracy feared was the bloodhounds which were set on his trail, and after he had shot these, his mind was more at ease.

After holding up another household of Johnsons, Tracy—accompanied by their hired man, Anderson, whom he forced to attend him as a human pack-horse—doubled back to Seattle by way of Port

Madison. He skirted the city till he came to South Seattle, and then cut around the end of Lake Washington to Renton. At this point he made himself the uninvited guest of the Jerrolds family. Walking up from Renton with his unwilling companion, Tracy met Miss May Baker, Mrs. McKinney, and young Jerrolds picking salmonberries. Tracy stopped them, smiling. "I guess you have heard of me; I am Tracy," he said; then added, "You needn't be afraid of me. I never harmed a woman in my life, and I don't intend to begin now."

Talking easily with the women, Tracy walked along to the house, in the rear of which he tied Anderson to a clump of bushes. He called the Jerrolds boy and handed him two watches, which he wished sold in order to buy two 45-calibre single-action Colt revolvers and a box of cartridges. He threatened to kill everybody in the house in case the boy betrayed him, but the lad was no sooner gone than he told Mrs. Jerrolds that this was mere bluff. This iron-nerved murderer and outlaw actually shed tears at this point.

"I wouldn't hurt you, Mother, for anything. I have a mother of my own somewhere back East. I haven't done just right by her, but I reckon all the mothers are safe from me, no matter what happens."

Presently Tracy brightened again and was laughing and talking with the three women just as if they had been old acquaintances. It was nearly time to prepare dinner, and Tracy carried in wood and volunteered to get the water from the spring. Rifle in hand, he sauntered down to the railroad track and filled his bucket with water. As he did so a special train, bearing the posse which hunted him, came round the bend. He ducked into the bushes to let it pass.

"I reckon there are some gentlemen in that train looking for me," he remarked carelessly when he had reached the house. "I saw a reporter there. They are always in the lead. First you see a reporter, then a cloud of dust, and after a while the deputies. It's the interviewer I'm afraid of!" And he laughed.

There was much gay talk and laughter during the meal which followed, in which Tracy took the lead. His repartee was apt and spirited, and his sallies were irresistible. The Jerrolds boy had informed the sheriff's officer of Tracy's whereabouts long ago, and by this time the deputies were beginning to surround the house. Everybody was alarmed save the outlaw himself. He strolled to the window and looked out at an enterprising photographer who was trying to take a picture of the house.

"My trousers are too short and they're not nicely ironed," he said. "I like to be neatly dressed before ladies. I guess I'll go out and hold up a deputy for a pair."

Miss Baker was worried in case she might not get home before dark. Tracy reassured her, saying it was a pleasant moonlit night, and that he would be glad to accompany her if he might have the pleasure.

As the day wore on the deputies gathered thicker and thicker around the house, cautiously drawing closer and closer, for they knew that the outlaw was a dead shot. Finally Tracy concluded that he had better be going. From his Chesterfieldian manner he might have been bidding his hostess good-bye after some elaborate function. From the back doorstep he waved them all a merry good day and wished them all manner of luck. As it happened, just at that moment poor Anderson had been discovered tied to a tree. One of the deputies gave a shout, and the others crowded round to see what was the matter. In the excitement Tracy quietly slipped down to the river and disappeared!

Day after day the chase after this extraordinary man continued. Hundreds of men beat the woods and patrolled the roads in vain. Once Tracy was wounded, but managed to keep under cover until he was again able to travel. He played hide-and-seek with the officers of King County for weeks, then suddenly broke away for the Cascades on horseback. Weeks later he turned up in eastern Washington en route for his old stamping ground, the "Hole-in-the-Wall" country. More than once his fondness for loitering for days in the same spot showed itself. His effrontery knew no bounds. At one place he made use of the telephone to call up a sheriff in order to tease him about his ill-success in capturing Tracy. Before he left, however, he gave the poor official one grain of consolation. "You've done better than the other sheriffs," he said. "You've talked with the man you want, anyway. Good-bye; I'm afraid you won't see me again."

But he did. Eastern Washington does not afford any such hiding ground as the big forests of the western part of the state. From point to point the telephone handed on the message that Tracy had just passed. He doubled here, there, and everywhere; but he could not shake off his relentless pursuers, aided as they were by the telephone wires. Sheriff Cudihee, now thoroughly aroused, swore never to leave the chase till Tracy was taken. Sheriffs Gardner and Doust and Cudihee held the passes and closed in on him.

Tracy had reached the rough country south of the Colville Indian reservation. He had become gaunt as an ill-fed wolf. Hunger, cold, and exposure have tamed more bad men than fear. They sap the physical well-being which in some men is the spring of courage. But they did not affect the iron nerve of his man. He was still as savage and as dangerous as on the day when he broke out of the penitentiary. For two days and nights the outlaw hung around the Eddy ranch, not far from Creston, until a young man who saw him there raced with the news to Sheriff Gardner, who hastened to the scene at once.

Meanwhile, a party of five citizens of Creston, which is in Lincoln County, stopped forever the evil career of the man who had travelled four hundred miles and baffled thousands of pursuers. C. C. Straub, deputy sheriff, Dr. E. C. Lanter, Maurice Smith, attorney, J. J. Morrison, section foreman, and Frank Lillen Green, all armed to the teeth, proceeded to the ranch of Mr. L. B. Eddy, where the outlaw was known to be in hiding. The country thereabout is very rocky, and the party took every care not to be

caught in an ambush. They saw Farmer Eddy mow-
ing his hay, and while talking with him observed a
strange man emerge from the barn.

"Is that Tracy?" asked one of them.

"It surely is," answered Eddy.

Eddy followed orders and drove to the barn.
Cautiously the members of the posse followed him.
Tracy came from the barn and began to help his host
unhitch the team. His rifle he had left in the barn,
but his revolvers he still carried. Suddenly he saw his
pursuers.

"Who are those men?" he demanded, turning
sharply to Eddy.

"Hold up your hands!" shouted the officers, without waiting for the farmer's reply.

Like a flash Tracy jumped behind Eddy and the
team and bade the terrified farmer lead the horses to
the barn. When near the door he made a break to
reach his rifle. A moment later he reappeared, rifle
in hand, and started headlong down the valley. Again
his iron nerve had brought him out of an apparently
certain trap. Two shots he fired at his pursuers, but
neither of them had effect.

The man hunters took up the chase at once. Tracy
dodged behind a rock and began firing rapidly. It
was growing dark, however, and he missed his men.
Then he made a dash for a wheat field near at hand,
the officers firing at him as he ran. Suddenly he stumbled and fell on his face, but dragged himself on
hands and knees into the field. He had been hit.

Sheriff Gardner and his posse now arrived on the

scene and surrounded the field. Presently a single shot was heard by the watchers. That shot sent the notorious bandit into eternity. In the early morning the cordon cautiously worked its way into the field and presently stumbled upon Harry Tracy's lifeless body. The most famous man hunt in the history of the country had ended. Crippled and bleeding, hopeless of escape, the bandit had shot himself sooner than let himself be taken.

After escaping from a dozen sheriffs, slipping cleverly out of death trap after death trap, and leaving behind him everywhere a trail of blood that would not have discredited an Apache chief, Tracy fell at last by his own hand rather than lose the liberty which he apparently prized more than life itself.

"FOUR SIXES TO BEAT——"

*Epitome of His Whole Reckless Career Were
These Last Words of John Wesley Hardin,
Peerless Texan Gun Ace*

"MR. HICKOK, meet Jack Hardin."

The scene was a wine room at Abilene, Kansas, the speaker a cattleman named Johnson, a trail driver who had just brought a herd up from the Guadalupe. The men whom he had just introduced looked straight into each other's eyes. One was a Northerner, the marshal of the town, the other was from Texas, a cowboy who had come to the trail's end with the longhorns.

Each man studied the other, trying to decide what was in the mind back of the steady gaze. For both of them were killers, and at any moment guns might flash. Hickok, marshal of Abilene, was generally recognized as the greatest gun fighter on the frontier. Privately Hardin disputed that. He was himself the most prodigal and notorious killer ever domiciled in the state of Texas, and he had come out of his own bailiwick quite prepared to discuss the other's supremacy if occasion offered.

"Wild Bill" Hickok was then in the prime of life, about thirty-four years of age, tall, erect, with long brown hair sweeping his broad shoulders. His nose was aquiline, his cheek bones high. For dress he affected the costume of the river gamblers—a dark, long-tailed cutaway, a fancy vest, blue trousers, narrow at the bottom and fastened to high-heeled boots polished like a mirror. Except when scouting he always wore a white shirt and black string tie. Supreme self-confidence, more than a hint of arrogance, was in his pose. He walked as lightly and as proudly as a buck in the rutting season. Why not? He was not only the most renowned fighting man of the West but by the testimony of dozens of contemporaries, including General Custer, Henry M. Stanley, and Colonel Little, he was voted one of the handsomest men who had ever swung a lithe body to the saddle. Colonel Nichols wrote that he was handsomer in face and form than he thought it possible for a mere man to be.

John Wesley Hardin made no such eye-filling spectacle as Hickok. He was of light complexion, five foot ten, and weighed about one hundred and fifty pounds. The dust of the trail was still on his cowboy costume. He was not bad-looking, but the eyes of women did not follow him down the street. After all he was only a gangling boy of nineteen, with light blue eyes, usually mild and quick to smile. To date he had killed only fifteen men, but he had no apologies to make for that. It was a much more imposing record than Hickok could have shown at his age. He stood at ease, as nonchalant as the older man.

Hickok spoke first. "I have a folder from Texas

in my pocket offering a reward for your arrest," he said.

"Are you arresting me?" Hardin asked quietly.

"Not now. Sit down and talk with me."

They took a table and ordered wine. Hickok made some inquiries about a fight on the Newton prairie, in the course of which Hardin had killed five Mexicans. The boy told the story.

"Young man, I am favourably impressed with you," Wild Bill said as he rose to go. "But don't let Ben Thompson influence you, for you are in enough trouble already. If I can do you any favour, let me know."

The reference to Ben Thompson needs explanation. The man was a notorious gunman and gambler. With Phil Coe (later killed by Wild Bill) he was running the Bull's Head saloon and gaming hall. A difference of opinion had arisen between them and the marshal, and it had resulted in enmity. As soon as Hardin reached town Thompson had sought him out and tried to prejudice him against Hickok.

"Bill is a Yank, and he always picks out Southerners, especially Texans, to kill," explained Thompson casually.

Hardin looked at him coolly. "I'm not doing anybody's fighting just now except my own, but I know how to stick to my friends," he said, in a slow drawl. "If Mr. Hickok needs killin', why don't you kill him yoreself?"

"I'm in business here. I'd rather get someone else to do it."

"You're talkin' to the wrong man," Hardin had answered.

Word had of course reached the marshal that the two men had been seen together. Hence his warning to Hardin.

But John Wesley Hardin was born to trouble as the sparks fly upward. He spent most of his time in Abilene in saloons and gambling houses, playing faro, poker, and seven-up. One day he and his friends grew too noisy, and the marshal came in. He told them to make less noise and ordered "Little Arkansaw," as he called Hardin, to take off his guns till he was ready to leave town.

"I'm ready to leave now, so I reckon I won't bother to take 'em off," the Texan answered.

Hickok turned away, and the boy followed him into the street. Someone gave a wild whoop. Wild Bill whirled on Hardin.

"What are you howling about? Why haven't you taken those pistols off?" he demanded.

"I'm just takin' in the town," Hardin answered.

What followed is in dispute. According to the autobiography of Hardin, Wild Bill drew a pistol.

"I arrest you. Take off those pistols," he said.

Then Hardin pulled the guns, reversed them swiftly, and held the marshal covered. The Texan made the other put up his weapon and cursed him for a coward and a scoundrel. A crowd gathered.

Wild Bill said the matter could be settled without trouble. Not for an instant did he lose his head, though he knew that the alternatives of life and death hung on the touch of a trigger finger. He talked the boy out of his impulse to kill—quietly, evenly, without raising his voice or showing the least fear.

"You're the quickest and the gamest boy I ever knew," he said. "Someone has been loadin' you, Little Arkansaw. I've never had any intention of shooting you in the back, as you say, or anywhere else. Why should I? Let's go in here and take a drink. I want to give you some advice."

At first the Texan was suspicious. He thought Wild Bill was looking for a chance to get the drop on him, but the older man convinced him of his sincerity. The two adjourned to the private room of a saloon, had a long talk, and came out friends.

This is Hardin's story. Those who knew Hickok well say that it cannot be true, since Wild Bill was not simple enough to let anyone roll his guns on him while being disarmed. The claim is made by others that Hardin was the first gunman to discover and perfect the "roll" and that the marshal was taken wholly by surprise, never having seen the trick before.

A few hours later Hardin and another Texan named Pain, who had just come up the trail, went into a restaurant for supper. Some drunken men entered, and one of them began to curse Texans.

Young Hardin spoke up, in the low soft drawl that predicated danger, "Two Texans present, meanin' me and my friend."

Guns were out and spitting lead in an instant. The stranger jumped behind Pain, who was a one-armed man. Pain was wounded. The stranger started to run, but Hardin's bullet struck him in the mouth and came out behind the left ear.

The young killer jumped over the prostrate man, ran to his horse, and galloped out of town. He rode to Cottonwood, thirty-five miles away, and waited there to see what would follow.

While John Wesley was on the dodge in the cow camps there a Mexican by the name of Bideno killed Billy Coran, a Texas cowman who had come up the trail with Hardin. Bideno escaped the posses that went after him. The cattlemen had Hardin appointed a deputy sheriff, and the young man took the trail at once. With him was Jim Rogers. It was sure that the Mexican would head for the Indian Nation, then a no-man's-land for criminals.

The pursuers rode fast, changing horses at different cow camps as they met trail herds. At Newton a brother of Coran and a cowboy named Anderson joined them. They passed Wichita, having ridden more than a hundred miles without hearing a word of the fugitive. Soon after this they picked up news of him from a Mexican cowman. During the day they heard of him frequently. He was going fast, but they were gaining on him. At Bluff Creek someone told Hardin that Bideno was in a restaurant eating. The Texan sauntered through the saloon into the eating house back of it.

Hardin ordered the fugitive to throw up his hands. Instead, Bideno reached for his weapon. The Texan's bullet hit him in the forehead, between the eyes.

Apparently Hardin felt that the Bideno business wiped out his misdemeanour of a few days before. He had heard that Wild Bill had threatened to kill him if he ever returned to Abilene. That was more than the Texan could stand. He went back to find out if this was true.

Wild Bill walked into the saloon where Hardin and his friends were celebrating. It was a gala occasion. The cattlemen had raised more than a thousand dollars as a reward for the killing of Bideno.

The marshal said, "Do you remember our talk in the Apple Jack? You can't hurrah me, if that's what you're here for. I won't have it."

"I don't want to hurrah you. I came back because I've a right to be here. That fellow in the restaurant tried to run on me."

"I've heard so," the marshal answered. "Well, I congratulate you on getting your Mexican. I'll break a bottle with you and your friends."

Everybody in the saloon had been waiting for the roar of guns, ready to dive for safety. Now the tension relaxed.

Hickok made the friends of Hardin take off their weapons, but allowed the young fellow to retain his, presumably because he was in danger from the friends of the man he had shot.

John Wesley had come up the trail with his four cousins, Jim, Manning, Joe, and Gip Clements. A few days after his return to Abilene Manning and Gip hunted him up.

Manning drew him aside. "Wes, I killed Joe and

Dolph Shadden last night, but I was justified," he said.

"Well, I'm glad you're satisfied, but I'm with you right or wrong," his cousin told him.

Manning had been bossing a trail herd for Doc Burnett and had hired the Shadden boys. According to Manning, they became lazy and insolent. All the way through the Nation they tried to stir up trouble. After crossing the Canadian they quit work entirely but stayed in camp. Manning offered them full pay to the end of the trail if they would leave.[1] They declined to go, and the talk in camp was that they meant to kill the boss. Manning slept away from the camp to avoid trouble until the Shaddens sneered at his cowardice. Then Manning knew it had come to a showdown. He returned to camp at night. The Shaddens were waiting for him. In the duel that followed he killed them both.

Hardin listened to his story. "I am a particular friend of Wild Bill, and I can fix it for you."

John Wesley was as good as his word. Hickok arrested Manning but gave the key of the jail to his cousin, who in turn handed it to Phil Coe. Soon Manning was astride a horse bound for his home in Texas. Hardin had promised to look after his young brother Gip.

Two days later Hardin killed a burglar who came

---

[1] This was Manning's story. There seems some reason to doubt it. He was one tough hombre, as dangerous a man as ever early Texas could boast, not the kind to give shirkers wages they had not earned. Manning Clement was killed in a saloon, shortly after the trial of John Selman for the murder of John Wesley Hardin. He had talked so freely that the anti-Hardin party decided it was best to get rid of him.

into his room at the American House to rob him. Half-dressed, Hardin and his cousin Gip slipped from the room to the hotel porch just as Wild Bill drove up in a hack to arrest him. After Hickok had gone into the hotel the two men dropped to the top of the hack, slipped inside it, and drove off.

The cousins separated. Hardin hid in a haystack. He could hear the officers discussing his whereabouts. From the haystack he crawled to a cornfield near. A cowboy passed close to him. Gun in hand, Hardin persuaded him to let him have the horse. The posse saw him mount and at once pursued. There was a hot race to the river. The hunted man's horse took the water and swam across.

Hardin reached a cow camp half an hour ahead of his pursuers. At once he borrowed a pair of trousers, two six-shooters, and a Winchester. He hid behind the river bank when Tom Carson, deputy marshal of Abilene, rode in with two companions. The Texan covered them and sent them back to town minus their weapons and their nether garments. He said it was only fair they should enjoy the pleasure he had had.

The Texan shook the dust of Kansas from his feet. He never again met Wild Bill or his deputy Tom Carson.

The life of Hardin offers to the psychologist interesting material for study. He was the son of a preacher, teacher, and lawyer, and he followed the paternal example so far as to study theology, teach school, and practise law. At one time he was the superintendent of a Sunday school. During his latter years in prison he seems honestly to have intended to lead a different life after he got out, but the pressure of circumstances was too much for his good resolution. He was a hard drinker, a gambler, a horse racer, a cowboy, a convict, and a killer who had slain six men before he was out of his fifteenth year. The man was daring to foolhardiness. Only an Apache could have equalled his stoicism. Callous and cold-blooded, he was none the less devoted to his family and loyal to his own clan. So faithful were his relatives that five or six of them went to death on account of their fidelity.

John Wesley Hardin was born at Bonham, Fannin County, Texas, May 26, 1853. His father was at that time a preacher, and though he voted against secession he joined the Confederacy and was captain of a troop. Young John Wesley grew up a rebel. The hatreds of the war were reflected in his life. During the reconstruction period he opposed bitterly the "carpetbag" régime. Yankee soldiers he seemed to consider legitimate game.

The first man he killed was a surly Negro named Mose. John Wesley and a cousin were matched to wrestle with the man. They threw him. He was not satisfied, and they threw him again. Accidentally they scratched his face and it bled. Mose became ugly and made threats. He was driven from the place. Young Hardin, on horseback carrying a message for his father, met him alone next day. Mose renewed hostilities. He cursed and threatened. The boy whipped the nag to a trot, but Mose seized the bridle and lashed at the rider with a stick. John Wesley drew a Colt .44 and shot him. The Negro plunged at him again and again, and each time the lad flung another bullet into him. Mose died within a few days. Texas was still under the rule of the carpetbaggers, and the boy became a fugitive.

His older brother Joe was teaching school on Logallis Prairie, twenty-five miles away. John Wesley joined him, spending most of his time hunting wild cattle. During the war cattlemen, away from home with the army, had not been able to brand the calves. As a result, there were now hundreds of thousands of unbranded cattle roaming the plains. The first man who got to them with a running iron became their owner.

The troops heard that John Wesley was on Logallis Prairie and they set out to capture him. He laid a trap for three of them, waiting in the bed of a deep creek. Two he killed with a double-barrelled shotgun, the third with his .44. He was himself wounded in the arm. Neighbours secreted and nursed him. Also, they buried the bodies of the troopers so effectively that the authorities never knew what had become of the missing men.

It was after this episode that young John Wesley taught school in Navarro County. He was scarcely sixteen years old, and he had both boys and girls as pupils who were his equal in age. But he was a natural leader, and none of them disputed his sway. At the end of a three-months' term he was offered a renewal contract, but he was eager to be a cowboy and turned his back on pedagogy.

There was wildness in his blood. It did not take him long to learn poker and seven-up after he had enrolled as a vaquero. In fact, he played the latter game so expertly that he became known as "Young Seven-Up." Racing was a favourite pastime of his. He was an inveterate bettor. Most of his associates were kinsfolk, of whom he had a great number. Among his cousins were Andersons, Dixons, Cunninghams, Clements, Barrickmans, and Milligans. Many of these were as reckless and as bold as he was, though none possessed his combination of cool courage, quiet effrontery, capacity for leadership, and skill with a six-shooter. A considerable number of them died violent deaths, as did their leader. His brother-in-law, Brown Bowen, was hanged by the law at Cuero in 1878 for the murder of Thomas Haldeman, insisting with his last words that John Wesley Hardin had committed the deed. Simp Dixon, implicated with John Wesley in the shooting of two Yankee soldiers, was cornered and shot to death at Cotton Gin. His two brothers, Tom and Bud, together with Joe Hardin, were hanged by a mob at Comanche after John Wesley Hardin and Bud Dixon had killed Charles Webb, a deputy sheriff. Manning Clements died with his boots on. So did others of Hardin's followers. They were a hard-riding, hard-drinking outfit, ready to shoot at the drop of the hat.

During those years while Hardin was building up

a reputation as Texas's worst bad man, he met at a race meet another killer who was ambitious to be chief. This was Bill Longley, destined to be the lad's greatest rival for the crown. Longley was a rough, harsh-spoken man, of the type that kills for the pleasure of it. The law terminated his career by hanging him October 11, 1879, for the murder of Wilson Anderson. It throttled him a few years too late to save the lives of a score of men.

John Wesley was a slim boy of seventeen when he met Longley, but he had long since learned that behind a six-gun he was a full-grown man. Longley attempted to bully him and failed. That evening the lad took $300 from him at poker.

Ben Hinds, another notorious desperado, was present at this same race meet. Young Hardin got into a game of seven-up with him on a dry-goods box and won $20, then decided to quit playing. Hinds lost his temper and said that if he was not a boy he would beat him to death. John Wesley was such a mild youth that bullies were likely to make a mistake.

"I stand in man's shoes," Hardin drawled. "Don't spoil a good intention because I'm a kid."

Hinds roared at him and started forward. He stopped. The youngster had him covered.

"I'm a little on the scrap myself," John Wesley told him. "Don't crowd, gentlemen. If I see any guns out this six-shooter is liable to go off."

Mr. Hinds looked into the cold steely eyes and decided to apologize. He had several friends with him, and this young Hardin sprout was alone, but—no use running on the prod, for if a fellow made a mistake he wouldn't ever have a chance to regret it.

Shortly after this Hardin was arrested at Waco for a crime which he claimed he did not commit. While being transferred to another town he killed his guard and escaped. He was taken prisoner again, this time by three police of the state force. Biding his time, he killed all three of them and made a getaway.

Texas was getting too warm for him. It was shortly after this that while on the dodge he had some difficulty with some Mexicans in a monte game. His own account of it is illuminating.

"My card came and I said, 'Pay the queen.' The dealer refused. I struck him over the head with my pistol as he was drawing a knife and shot another. Well, this broke up the monte game, and the casualties were a Mexican with his arm broken, another shot through the lungs, and one with a sore head. We all went back to camp and laughed about the matter."

This was in February, 1871, just before he started on his famous trip to Abilene with his cousins, the Manning brothers.

Upon his return to Texas he killed a Negro member of the state police named Green Paramoor. He justified this on the ground that these troops were made up "of carpetbaggers and scalawags from the North, with ignorant Negroes frequently on the force." Instead of protecting life, liberty, and property they destroyed them, according to Hardin.

While still a boy in years he married Jane Bowen. This did not change his swashbuckling ways. He continued to be constantly in trouble. In a duel with Phil Sublet both of them were wounded. Two months later Hardin was wounded again by two members of the police force who had come to arrest him. One of these he killed.

He was in a desperate plight. Scores of troopers were looking for him, and he was troubled by old and new wounds. He sent a friend to the sheriff of Cherokee County, Dick Reagan, to say that he would surrender upon a guarantee of protection from a mob. Terms were arranged. John Wesley reached for the revolver under the pillow to give to Reagan. A deputy mistook the gesture and shot the wounded man through the knee. The prisoner was taken to Rusk with four bullet holes in him.

By this time Hardin had killed thirty men, and he was an object of curiosity. Many visitors, both men and women, came to see him. They were surprised at his mild, harmless appearance. "He looks just like we'uns," they would say to one another.

Hardin was taken to Austin and from there to Gonzales. He escaped from prison by cutting the iron bars. Manning Clements and another friend were waiting outside for him with horses.

It must have been apparent that Hardin was near the end of his rope. There was a strong public sentiment against him, but he did not reform. He killed J. B. Morgan over some trifling disagreement. Later he was tried for this, pleaded guilty of manslaughter, and was given a two-year sentence. But this was several years after the killing.

A feud between the Suttons and the Taylors broke out and was fought with great bitterness. Hardin and his friends joined the Taylors. John Wesley shot down Jack Helms, sheriff of De Witt County. A month or two later he slew Charles Webb, deputy sheriff of Brown County.

This was the last straw. The Rangers brushed the country for Hardin. Now with one of his friends, now with another, he had a dozen remarkable escapes from capture. Those allied with him did not fare so well. His brother Joe, now a well-established lawyer, was hanged by a mob side by side with two of his cousins, Bud and Tom Dixon. Two other cousins, Aleck Barrickman and Ham Anderson, were surrounded and shot to death by Rangers. Scrap Taylor, Tuggle, and White, cowboys associated with Hardin, were lynched a few weeks later.

Hardin escaped from the country. He went to New Orleans and from there to Gainesville, Florida. He moved to Jacksonville. The Pinkertons tracked him down. He got out in time, heading for New Orleans. The detectives were close at heel. In a fight he and a companion shot down two. Other Pinkerton men took up the chase. Hardin was surprised in a railroad coach and arrested after a desperate hand-to-hand encounter, during which one of the men with him was killed.

The notorious prisoner was taken back to Texas. All the way people crowded the stations to get a glimpse of him. He was tried for the murder of Charles Webb and given twenty-five years in the penitentiary.

John Wesley Hardin had killed his last man. By his own admission he had slain thirty-five. Others can probably he added to this list, for there were reasons why in some cases he did not want to involve himself. But for a youth of twenty-five this is an appalling record, probably the largest authenticated one of any of the Western killers.

There is a great deal of exaggeration among those who write of the records of gunmen. One writer says that Bat Masterson killed thirty men at Dodge. This is absurd. According to Burns, the author of *Tombstone*, Wyatt Earp puts the total number killed by Bat at four. Charley Duesha is said by one recorder to have got more than twenty men in the Tonto Basin war. In all there were about twenty-four or twenty-five slain during that sanguinary feud, and there must have been forty or fifty men engaged in the war. The record of Wild Bill is largely guesswork. The same is true of Billy the Kid and Jesse James. Therefore the thirty-five which John Wesley Hardin sets down in his autobiography as victims of his marksmanship—sets down chronologically, with dates and names appended—is a longer list than can be gathered in the case of any other killer. I do not mean to say that Hardin ended the earthly careers of more men than did Wild Bill or Jesse James. Probably this is not the case. His record is better known. For instance, Mark Twain says in *Roughing It* that Slade, whom he met while crossing the plains, had killed twenty-eight men. Since Twain met him while the memory of his deeds was fresh there must be some justification for his statement. But the historian to-day digging into the past can give the name of only one man slain by Slade.

Mr. Hardin was taken to the penitentiary and there had plenty of time to reflect upon the error of his ways. He was twenty-five when he went in. He was forty-one when he came out, pardoned by Governor Hogg of Texas. In his early years at Huntsville Hardin was not a philosopher. He was not even a model prisoner. It is not too much to say that he was one of the most unruly ever confined in a penitentiary.

He began at once to plot an escape. The warden had assigned him to work at the wheelwright's shop. About twenty-five yards from this the armoury was situated. He took in as accomplices about seventy-five other prisoners, most of them long-time men. They tunnelled through five brick walls each two feet thick, using saw bits, chisels, and knives. The work was finished, but just before the jail break some life convicts betrayed the conspirators. Hardin was put in a dark cell and given bread and water for fifteen days.

As soon as he was taken back to work he planned another attempt at escape. Just before the time for putting it into execution he was seized and searched. Once more he had been betrayed.

He was mercilessly flogged with a heavy whip that left his back and sides a quivering jelly. He would confess nothing, and even under that horrible torture defied the guards and told them he would kill them if they stood in the way of his escape. He was a sick man for months, and as soon as he had recovered began plotting another attempt to win his liberty.

The early years of his incarceration were filled with plots, betrayals, and floggings. He refused to work and was put into a tank into which water poured and could only be kept down by pumping. Hardin would not pump. The water closed over his head and he would have drowned if the keepers had not dragged him out and resuscitated him.

After a time there came a change over the man. He began to read, to study mathematics and history. He gave a good deal of attention to theology, ran the prison Sunday school, and was prominent in the debating society. Mr. Hardin was by way of becoming a model prisoner.

It was about this time that he writes his wife of having spent a day of almost perfect happiness in his cell, though it was some years later that he fathered the following excellent though ungrammatical maxim: "If you wish to be successful in life, be temperate and control your passions; if you don't, ruin and death is the inevitable result."

After he had been in prison about seven years Hardin decided to study law and wrote to the superintendent asking for advice as to the best procedure. A prominent lawyer in Hunstville recommended textbooks, and the prisoner set to work reading Blackstone, Kent, Storey, and Greenleaf.

Hardin was pardoned by Governor Hogg and full citizenship restored to him March 16, 1894. Still in his early forties, John Wesley Hardin had visions of making himself a good and useful citizen. Shortly before his release Mrs. Hardin had died. The ex-convict settled at Gonzales and there took up the practise of law. He married again in 1895.

Unfortunately Hardin became involved in a bitter newspaper controversy over an election. The man he opposed was elected. He moved to Karnes County and from there to El Paso. He was finding it hard to get a foothold in the law. It is said that he moved to El Paso because that city was a wide-open town, still riotous with the exuberant life of the frontier which in his youth had so appealed to Hardin.

From the first it became apparent that the move to El Paso was unfortunate. The mayor of the city called upon him and served notice that if he made any trouble he would be killed first and the cause investigated later. John Selman and George Scarborough quarrelled over which one was to have the privilege of "settling the hash" of Mr. Hardin. The newcomer became weary of well-doing and took to drinking and gambling. He and his young wife had separated. Perhaps that was why he became involved with another woman. The husband of the woman was assassinated. Who committed the murder is not known.

Time had taken its toll of John Wesley's fighting fire. He had trouble with two rising and ambitious gunmen and showed a desire to compromise the trouble. Later, perhaps to bolster his reputation, he held up a game in a saloon and walked out with his pockets full of money. He was arrested and released on bond.

Then, unfortunately for him, he fell foul of John Selman, who was a law officer at El Paso and a killer of note. The cause of the quarrel was unimportant. A son of Selman, a policeman, had arrested the woman in whom Hardin was interested, Hardin was unarmed when he and John Selman met. The officer told him, after hot words, to get heeled.

According to Selman, Hardin answered, "When I meet you I'll come a-smoking and make you pull like a wolf around the block."

A little later Hardin was in the Acme saloon shaking dice with an acquaintance. Selman came into the place. Hardin was facing the bar, his back to the officer.

To his friend, Hardin said. "Four sixes to beat."

Selman shot him in the back of the head and then twice in the body. At his trial he later testified that Hardin saw him in the looking glass back of the bar and started to reach for a gun. Selman was defended ably by A. B. Fall, later Secretary of the Interior, and was acquitted.

Eight months later John Selman was shot down in a gun duel by George Scarborough. Selman was then about fifty-eight years old and had lived a stormy life. Bass Outlaw, a deputy United States marshal, was one of the men he had killed. On one occasion he fought a band of cattle thieves in Donna Ana

County, New Mexico, killing two and capturing the rest of the gang.

Scarborough was in turn shot down by Kid Curry of Arizona, who later passed out to the sound of roaring guns. So in each case the Scripture was fulfilled, that he who takes the sword shall perish by it.

THE END